S0-AEB-729

RESIDENTIAL SOCIAL WORK
General Editor: Tom Douglas

Group Living

Group Living

THE APPLICATION OF GROUP DYNAMICS
IN RESIDENTIAL SETTINGS

Tom Douglas

TAVISTOCK PUBLICATIONS

LONDON and NEW YORK

First published in 1986 by
Tavistock Publications Ltd
11 New Fetter Lane
London EC4P 4EE

Published in the USA by
Tavistock Publications
in association with Methuen, Inc.
29 West 35th Street, New York
NY 10001

© 1986 Tom Douglas

Typeset by
Scarborough Typesetting Services
and printed in Great Britain by
Richard Clay
(The Chaucer Press) Ltd
Bungay, Suffolk

All rights reserved. No part of this
book may be reprinted or
reproduced or utilized in any form or
by any electronic, mechanical or
other means, now known or
hereafter invented, including
photocopying and recording, or in
any information storage or retrieval
system without permission in writing
from the publishers.

British Library Cataloguing in
Publication Data

Douglas, Tom
Group living: the application of
group dynamics in residential
settings.
– (Residential social work) –
(Social science paperback; 328)
1. Social groups
I. Title   II. Series   III. Series
302.3   HM131

ISBN 0–422–79490–2

Library of Congress Cataloging in
Publication Data

Douglas, Tom.
Group living.
(Residential social work)
(Social science paperbacks; 328)
Bibliography: p.
Includes indexes.
1. Institutional care.
2. Small groups.
3. Social groups.
I. Title
II. Series: Social science
paperbacks; 328.
HV59.D68 1986   361.4   86–5832

ISBN 0–422–79490–2 (pbk.)

Contents

To Shirley with love and grateful thanks
for all her help and encouragement.

1 Introduction

'From another angle, group living constitutes a situation decidedly different from family living. First, unlike family living it has no single, continuous, unifying cultural history for the members involved. Its quality is primarily determined by the immediate existing group structure, group processes, and group properties such as membership composition, ongoing interpersonal relationships, and the overall socio-emotional climate of the group. In other words in the absence of a substantial common past and an extended joint future history, group living is essentially shaped by those group factors that decide the history of any group, notably the ongoing group members' interactions, their joint history in problem-solving, and their immediate effectiveness in contributing to each other's individual growth and mutual interdependence. It is reasonable to suggest, therefore, that group living is not institutionalized living, but a group in operation.'

(Maier 1961: 124)

Maier has in this quotation succinctly stated the whole purpose of this book; that is, to regard the residential establishment as a group organization and to pick from the available knowledge of the way groups perform those facets that seem to be of greatest relevance to the residential scene. My only quibble with Maier's statement would be that the last phrase should read '. . . but *groups* in operation', for the simple reason that although a residential system can be referred to as a 'group' it is often an organization containing many groups. Thus the first section of this introductory chapter is concerned with the nature of small groups, because these entities are the prime instrument of our analysis of the residential establishment.

So much has been written about groups in the last thirty years that an aura of 'specialness' has grown up about them. The very idea of being able to understand the patterns of relationships between a number of people, which are in any case constantly (or apparently so) changing and developing in the context of what the group is trying to achieve, seems a task of Herculean complexity to the beginner. We must, therefore, attempt to bring the concept of 'groupness' into the general run of everyday life where it truly belongs and emphasize that it is only because groups are fundamentally interesting that they have been studied in minute detail. When this occurs with any 'natural' phenomenon what emerges is frequently unrecognizable in its analysed state. This has something to do with the kind of language that investigators use to describe their work, but it is also because apparently simple processes like the development of familiarity between members of a group are in reality interactive and extremely complex, with multiple networks of relationships involved.

The second section of this chapter looks briefly at the nature of the research on, and writing about, small groups. It is my contention that to offer possible explanations about the behaviour of groups without presenting something about the nature and quality of the material from which they derive is no better than making assertions from pure whim. As we shall see, the general run of social research is so constrained by the complexity of its subject material, and by the adoption of the scientific method to a subject area which does not respond very well to such an investigative approach, that at best the results need to be tested in practice and substantiated by experience, and at worst they are interesting but practically inapplicable. However, there is quite a collection of tested hypotheses of proven use (M. E. Shaw in 1971 produced 105 such pieces of substantiated data), and the number is growing. Some pieces are included in this book because I have found them stimulating and because they square with what I would expect. They should be treated with some degree of caution until personally substantiated.

The third section is concerned with the residential scene and is of necessity somewhat general. Specific examples from different kinds of setting will be used where possible; but because the range of residential institutions is so wide, I have attempted to draw general concepts applicable in some degree to all settings. They all have many factors in common (see Douglas 1983: 158–76).

In trying to show how the research and writing about groups can be a valuable knowledge resource and the basis for enhanced practice, we need to look at the concept of 'consequences'. If there is to be any logical improvement of practice then it is essential that the causal relationship between doing something and the long- and short-term consequences should not only be known about but also monitored, recorded, and eventually analysed. Only in this way can data be formulated into working hypotheses that have the backing of records to show the nature of the cause/effect sequence. It is this kind of knowledge alone that underwrites good – that is, effective – practice.

THE NATURE OF SMALL GROUPS

'The misconception which has haunted philosophic literature throughout the centuries is the notion of independent existence. There is no such mode of existence. Every entity is only to be understood in terms of the way it is interwoven with the rest of the universe.'

(A. N. Whitehead, quoted in Hughes 1980: 32)

As we shall see later, this statement applies with great force to the idea about groups that we shall call 'embedding'. Here it suffices to introduce the basic nature of 'groupness'; i.e. that while we recognize the individual and the element of intelligent control that he or she may exert, we must primarily acknowledge the fact that each individual has largely been formed by group interaction and is continuously held in a complex matrix of social groupings past and present, which serve to maintain him or her in a state of personal equilibrium.

This fact is not commonly recognized until some form of social crisis occurs, even of an ordinary nature like changing jobs. The sense of anxiety about the new job is in effect a realization that there is little here that is familiar, little that can be predicted, including the kind of response that will be evoked in others. What has happened is that a whole supportive and familiar network of an interactive kind has been given up in order to gain certain advantages. Along with those gains goes the necessity of creating, over time, a new and potentially supportive mesh of relationships. If the old network has been too constraining or restricting, too unexciting or lacking in imagination, then the chance to build new networks might be one of the major advantages of change.

By now the first basic assertion about the nature of groups must be evident, which is that there is nothing mysterious or even new about them. From the moment of birth to that of death we are part of a complex social system of groups, the influence of which is ever present, often long after the group itself has ceased to exist as such. For example, the members of a family may be scattered over the face of the earth, and some members may be dead, but the influence of the family as a group is very strong, largely because its influence was created during those years of early life when dependence was at its greatest.

If we all know about groups, if we are all shaped by groups well or badly, if we are all continuously influenced by the groups of which we are members, why all the fuss about groups? The answer is contained in the question. It is precisely because the whole of life is 'group life' that the influence of groupings, transient or permanent, is regarded as 'natural' like breathing. Like breathing, the essential nature of group influence becomes mainly noticeable when either it creates problems or its function becomes erratic or abnormal. Like breathing also, most people would regard paying attention to group influence as unnecessary on the grounds that 'it seems to be working well enough'. But as health specialists continually assert, we can control our breathing with great beneficial effect to our health.

The factor of choice enters here. If an individual has no knowledge that it is possible to control his or her breathing — that is, he or she is wholly under the impression that it is an automatic process which functions reasonably well without conscious effort or interference on his or her part – then he or she will make no effort to control it. A choice that is available to the person in theory is no choice at all because he or she does not know of its existence.

The same is wholly true of the influence that groups exert on the behaviour of their members. Where the influence attempt is open and understood as such, then choice in the matter of response is possible even if the choices are highly unpalatable. It then becomes a matter of preference based upon the existing perception the individual has of the situation. Thus although all of us are in a way experts at setting up and responding to group pressures in what are called 'naturally' occurring groups, there is no doubt that many of our responses have become habits, set up at earlier periods of our lives and triggered by the perception of certain kinds of situation without the intervention of any form of conscious thought. The whole process of studying group behaviour is to create the possibility of increasing the element of conscious choice rather than of automatic response in those areas of life where choice is a crucial element of being human, and also to create groups for others where the same kind of increase in choice over behavioural responses to group pressures is possible. Thirdly, a knowledge of group processes is essential to any real understanding of individual behaviour, because the behaviour of the individual is often largely, though not often wholly, a response to the pressures of those groups of which he or she is a member.

As we shall see in the next section, this powerful interest in the ways in which the presence of others affects behaviour has created some problems. For instance, to study the so-called 'naturally' occurring groups is almost impossible. The observer, if visible, tends to generate an effect upon the group members; they know they are being watched and become self-conscious. To the extent that the outcome of the observation process might be important to them, they will modify their 'normal' behaviour according to their perception of their need to influence that outcome one way or another.

It is possible to study observer effect and to discount it as a major factor. It is possible also for the observer to become an accepted member of the group he or she is studying. But being accepted means conforming to the normal patterns of group behaviour and thus influencing outcomes. This entails some considerable loss of observer objectivity.

For all these reasons and others, observers have tended to set up experimental groups or to create experimental situations with 'natural' groups. Here the bias is of a different nature, in that the former groups have no continuing existence apart from the duration of the experiment, and in the latter a degree of artificiality or deviousness is necessarily introduced into an otherwise ongoing 'natural' situation. However, because certain patterns of behaviour tend to emerge with great regularity in all forms of group observation, it is possible to put together a fairly comprehensive catalogue of the ways in which groups tend to influence the behaviour of their members.

One more point needs to be made here about the nature of small groups. All groups of human beings display the same patterns of behaviour. This needs some clarification. Some groups display very few behavioural patterns, and some display a great deal; some display patterns at a high level of intensity, others very weakly; some produce certain patterns with great frequency, and others hardly at all. The process is not so much that the groups are essentially different in some fundamental sense like fire and water, but that they combine the same basic ingredients in a multitude of different ways. The difference between groups is much more like the difference between breeds of dogs than that between dogs and fish.

Ultimately a group is any collection of human beings that coalesces for a period of time, however brief. No matter how much we may need to look at very specific forms of groups, it should not be forgotten that they all belong to the same family and that a basic understanding of the dynamics of groups will give access to some understanding of all groups.

'A comprehensive definition of "groups" can be formulated in terms of the following properties: interaction between individuals, perceptions of other members and the development of shared perceptions, the development of affective ties, and the development of interdependence of roles.'

(DeLamater 1974: 39)[1]

THE NATURE OF SMALL-GROUP RESEARCH AND WRITING

'It is essential for the practitioner of social treatment to have some understanding of the theories that underlie his practice. This is so not only because it is from theory that strategies of treatment are derived, but also because implicit in each theory is a value orientation and view of man which may have a profound effect on the nature of the helping service delivered by the professional.'

(Whittaker 1974: 262)

Some of the problems concerned with small-group research and writing have already been mentioned in the previous section. An examination of what is available is now in order to assess the quality of the information on offer to the residential practitioner.

Let us be clear, first of all, that no satisfactory theory of group behaviour exists. There are many partial theories of, for instance, the beginnings of groups; of the developmental sequence; of group processes; of group leadership, etc. There are also many approaches to the understanding and use of groups, which are based upon an interpretative use of some of the major theories of general psychology like Freudian concepts, Gestalt, behaviourist, and humanistic ideas. There are major disagreements between theoreticians and between practitioners who tend to declare all work that is not similar to their own as of little consequence or absurd. But out of this welter of cross-purposes emerges some research that attempts the almost impossible task of seeking the similarities in the material rather than the differences, on the basis that, if various researchers and writers from highly disparate starting points can be seen to be describing similar phenomena, then the chances are that these phenomena exist in some real sense.

There are nevertheless problems of language. Seldom if ever do researchers and writers of different persuasions describe what they see in the same terms. So the 'synthesizers' must spend a great deal of time and effort ascertaining the degree of correlation that exists between the variables being researched or written about.

In the main, then, research and writing about small groups fall into several categories, each with a particular contributive value to the practitioner. Nearly all need some form of translation into practice implications before that value can begin to be realized. The categories are as follows.

(1) Experimental groups

These are specifically set up to monitor the effects of a fragment of group behaviour. As far as possible the experiment is established in such a way that the effect being monitored can be isolated, and some attempt is made to measure it. Also, as a safeguard against measuring something that would have occurred anyway without the introduction of the special stimulus being tested, a control group is used, as similar in all respects as possible to the experimental one, to which nothing is done except monitor its responses over the same period as the experimental group. Material from this kind of research often corroborates common sense; but often also its findings are biased by the 'experimental' nature of the groups used (e.g. having no existence outside of the needs of the experimenter) and are only marginally useful in practice because of (a) the general nature of the findings and (b) the usually very limited and specific area of behaviour examined.

(2) Experimental sequences introduced into pre-existing groups

This situation occurs when the investigator takes an existing group, deliberately inserts into the group some factor he or she thinks will produce a result, and then attempts to measure the result in terms of its relationship to the artificially induced stimulus. The whole basis of the Mayo–Roethlisberger experiments at the Hawthorne Works was of this nature, when the working conditions of a group were changed and the effect was measured in terms of the changes in production levels. There are many problems associated with this kind of work, not least that the cause/effect between induced stimulus and measured change may be neither direct nor even causally related at all. It is also possible that differences of perception between the investigator and group of the nature of the stimulus offered can crucially affect the outcome.

(3) Direct observation

This can take place in one of two ways: either as a member of a group or as an outsider. In either case, as mentioned earlier, the problems of being seen to be present and of loss of objectivity through conforming to group norms are present. There is also a problem of an ethical nature if the observer is hidden from the group.

(4) Recordings or case studies

These are often very illuminating if available over a good period of the group's history, but they suffer from the general fault of such material that it relates to a unique situation. True, there will always be an element of similarity that all groups possess, but such material needs to be directly comparable with other studies on a vast scale before any general patterns can be said to exist with certainty.

(5) Synthesis

It is just this matter of comparability that makes the work of synthesists so necessary. The problem here is that of finding likes to compare, and because of this difficulty the material that finally emerges is usually of a banal nature.

(6) Analysis of experience

In some ways this means taking personal experience, using theoretical material and converting it into practical techniques, and then noting the results. Once more, this is susceptible to the unique nature of personal experience, but it does tend to provide more evidence for the synthesis approach.

When we come to examine group structure later (Chapter 3), we will see that it is possible to consider it in terms of frequency of occurrence. That is also the way in which most of the available knowledge about group behaviour comes to be accepted. Certain patterns are found to exist in all forms of writing about groups; they can be recognized by people who know little about group dynamics, and there is adequate evidence that they can be used to form the basis for effective techniques of acquiring understanding of group behaviour and for working with groups.

Some of this kind of material will be used here, as well as other research and writing that has not got a similar level of validity gained over a long period of time, but tends to support commonly held ideas or gives perhaps the only insight available into some aspects of group behaviour. Such material is more suspect and needs confirmation from other sources, but the level of risk is probably worth taking where information is indeed scarce. 'Social research of any kind is advanced by ideas; it is only disciplined by fact' (C. Wright-Mills 1959, quoted in Schur 1979: 3).

THE NATURE OF THE RESIDENTIAL SETTING: GROUP LIVING

It seems to be generally believed that a residential setting means that accommodation is provided in some vaguely benevolent way. It means the provision of somewhere to live that is other than what the person so accommodated would have lived in had circumstances proved different. Because it is seen as accommodation, i.e. a roof over one's head, the temptation is to think of it in the same mode of thought as so-called 'normal' living – that is, as if it were living in the normal course of events. Just as few people have ever regarded their family or work group or friendship group in terms of group interaction (largely because it has never occurred to them to think of it in this way), so few ever think of a residential establishment as a multiple group system, but that is what it is. It would perhaps be more correct to say that it is very productive of understanding to regard a residential establishment as a multiple group system.

Those who work in such systems are faced with practical situations giving them little time to consider how the information that is available about the ways in which people behave in such situations could be of value. Indeed many have an abhorrence of what they call 'theory', primarily because the links between information and its practical use have never been properly forged. This is a pity for many reasons, namely:

(1) There is much more information available that is reasonably well founded on factual data than anyone ever uses.
(2) The practical value of this information has not been effectively demonstrated, though it could be.
(3) Thus each work situation has to be dealt with on the basis of its uniqueness, as situations and techniques are seldom recorded or transferred.
(4) Progress towards a body of available knowledge is very slow.
(5) Traditional approaches perpetuate mistakes as well as good practice.
(6) Practice is often based on rule-of-thumb, which means that the basic principles underlying such behaviour are seldom learned. If they were, then a sound basis for a creative and imaginative response to situations would be available.

The use of a residential setting for specific aspects of living is as old as humanity itself. Even the use of such systems for special purposes has a long and chequered history. Fundamentally a residential institution is exactly what it is supposed to be, a place to live; but as most people in our society have somewhere to live that is not a residential institution in any true sense of the phrase, then other facets of a definition need to be explored.

Leaving aside those residential systems that are connected with religious practices (and even these possess all the qualities that will be listed below), the major reason for any residential institution is that it provides for some need of society or of individuals either that they cannot meet for themselves or that facilitates some process which cannot be maintained by any other means. This covers the whole gamut of human need, from basic companionship to being cut off from the mainstream of society; it includes learning, treatment, and all forms of care. This is an enormously wide range, all such institutions having points in common that make it possible to talk about a residential system.

The points in common are obvious enough; residential institutions all:

(1) provide some form of living-in situation;
(2) group together under one roof people with no ordinary relationship to each other apart from being human and having a common need or needs;
(3) define boundaries and access and create a set of rules that is different in some respects to the norms of society; they also restrict the element of choice;
(4) process people by having operational goals, e.g. to socialize, to learn, to get better;
(5) provide the staple necessities for staying alive;
(6) usually have clear distinctions between those who operate the system, whatever it may be, and those who are the subjects of the operation.

In addition:

(7) all, or nearly all, are part of a much larger system or organization, which has wider and more diffuse goals than the residential unit.

Some are total institutions in that the whole period of the individual's connection with the system is spent within it; others are partial. Some serve a brief containment function, perhaps with repeated entry and discharge, while others keep their residents for very long periods of time. Nevertheless all these institutions bring together a collection of assorted individuals and work with them to attain prescribed and socially desirable ends. This definition, without the overall concept of residency, would fit very closely almost any form of group. It is my contention, therefore, that the mass of available material about group behaviour should contain much that is relevant to residential work. Indeed, as we shall see, residential settings are often the venue for specially created groups of residents, groups that are directly comparable in all respects to all other 'created' groups, except for the facts of the environment in which they exist and the restriction on the numbers of the population from which the members are chosen.

In their book *Group Care for Children*, Ainsworth and Fulcher define group living as 'small residential units existing within the community designed to meet the many criticisms which have been directed at the large institutions for some time' and to 'provide care, protection and training . . . on a personalised scale' (1981: 6). While this is a valid definition of the term, especially in view of the authors' concern to establish the concept of 'group care', I would want it to encompass also the larger residential establishments, for reasons that will emerge clearly during the discussion on embedding (see Chapter 7). It is much more difficult to see the seepage of influence between groups when studying a collection of individuals that not only is small enough to be regarded as a unitary group but tends to be treated as such. In this context, then, the term 'group living' is taken to apply to all residential situations both large and small.

THE RELATIONSHIP OF VALUE ONE TO THE OTHER

In chapter 9 of *Groups: Understanding People Gathered Together* (Douglas 1983), I began an analysis of residential institutions in terms of group processes. This form of analysis, if pushed further, can provide a basis for residential workers to develop an enhanced understanding of some of the processes that, whether known about or not, inevitably affect not only the outcomes of their daily work, but the quality of it and of their achievement levels.

My belief that this is so has been sustained and enhanced by many contacts with people working in residential and other organizational settings, who in workshops and in discussion have brought up problems so obviously related to a limited and limiting understanding of the processes at work in their situation. What emerges from these contacts is that the starting point for an enhanced ability to cope is a clear recognition of the nature of the problems faced. That problems exist is abundantly clear, but for various reasons, which will be discussed later, they are not always seen for what they are. Behaviour is often ascribed by observers to the perceived personality of the individual producing it – e.g. 'He or she is a bad-tempered so-and-so' – whereas the actor is more likely to describe what he or she did as a response to his or her perception of the situation. This is a very frequent cause of conflict in all manner of situations, which some understanding of the nature of person perception might well help to reduce.

Because much residential work is concerned with the management of people, which requires the exercise of leadership skills, and because the skills of being a leader are a fundamental part of group processes, an analysis of those group factors that are extensively and intensively operative in residential situations should yield material of interest to residential workers. Take the fact of attempting to bring about change in an organizational structure. The idea of change and the design of the change may be highly desirable and can be thought about almost in isolation from the organization itself. But the implementation of that change can be brought about effectively only if a clear understanding of the dynamics of the system it is proposed to change is in existence. 'Dynamics of the system' does not mean here the roles, status, and responsibility of those who comprise the system, though they are important; rather, what should be known is how each person in that system perceives it, his or her relationship to it and to the others within it. If this is not known, then however good and ultimately beneficial the proposed change may be as judged by an impartial observer, it will be only partially acceptable at best to those whose enthusiastic co-operation is needed to make it work. Why is this so? Largely, I think, because their perception of what is happening looks wholly different from where they stand because of personal factors, and is thus an individualized reading of the nature of things, to the view of the pushers of change. They are not wrong, nor necessarily bloody-minded; they just have a personal slant.

One of the main lessons that working with groups teaches is that the personal slants of group members will operate in obscurity to influence group outcomes unless such 'hidden agendas' as are relevant to the situation in which the group is currently engaged are made known and thus can be taken into account.

This is no easy task. What is it that frees people from the fear of appearing to look foolish, ignorant, or both? What is it that makes them realize that their hidden agendas are possibly of great importance to the group? The answer from studies of group behaviour would seem to be that it is necessary for members of a group to have a sense that what they do will be accepted by their peers without diminution of the respect and affection of the group for them. Even in everyday life the development of such a perception by members of a group takes a considerable time to develop. It is built upon the accumulation of experience in the context of the group, which tends to produce evidence that to behave in certain ways produces certain kinds of response, that these responses are probably changing away from the suspicion and self-protection towards more openness, sincerity, and supportiveness. It is built upon a realization by each member that perhaps they can venture or risk just a little more, which if successfully achieved adds another example to the growing list for all members of what is acceptable; this will tend to encourage equal involvement and perhaps increased participation on their part.

The value, then, of the application of knowledge about group behaviour to residential systems is, or could be, inestimable. A society can be generated in which the rules of behaviour developed will be those that are most supportive of residents, based upon a thorough understanding of how groups come to develop such norms. The concepts of public conformity and private acceptance (see Chapter 4) will allow the difference to be recognized between an acceptance of the group norms based upon the need to survive and one based upon a whole-hearted agreement with them.

Behaviour that is often attributed to individualistic responses, to personality defects, to sheer awkwardness, or even to attention-seeking can spring from group motivation. To respond to the individual, and to ignore the group influences that generated the energy for the behaviour and sponsored it, is to create a sense amongst group members that no understanding of them or their behaviour exists, and on the part of the individual of downright injustice. Both these factors tend to develop into self-fulfilling prophecies whose influence is not limited to the areas where understanding is obviously lacking but also taint and diminish the areas of previous solid achievement.

There is so much that can be missed about the causes of behaviour which stems from treating a group or groups as if they were collections of separate individuals who just happen to be in the same place at the same time. Even at this level, the awareness of the presence of others and the perception of the value of these others – the need that may exist for their approval, hatred, or disapproval, their acceptance no matter what – powerfully affects which of his or her repertoire of learned-through-experience behaviour is produced by each individual. For this reason we must end this introductory chapter with a brief discussion of consequences.

It is a fascinating thought that so much of our attempt to understand human behaviour is historical and causative, two areas where any attempt to acquire the quality of information required even to make informed guesses is almost impossible. Yet we can easily see the immediate consequences of behaviour even though we may not have the remotest idea why a response takes the form that it does. In residential settings it is also often possible to see the long-term consequences of behaviour because residents are together for long periods of time. Causes are almost always speculative; consequences are almost always visible.

One fact that I hope will emerge with startling clarity from the material in this book is the interrelated nature of all parts of the discussion. For instance, in considering the problems of accepting newcomers into an already established group – an almost everyday experience in a residential situation – the material covered under the subheading 'Safety' (p. 81) is immediately relevant. Not only that; virtually every other aspect of the knowledge of group behaviour can be seen to have something to contribute. In taking a phenomenon like a group to pieces in order to examine in detail some of its important manifestations, we are in great danger of endowing those parts with an independent existence. One of the major issues of this book is to show that such an approach guarantees a less than adequate understanding of group phenomena. Nothing can be understood effectively if it is taken out of context. So, although the structure of a book requires that the parts of a subject shall be examined in turn, every effort will be made here to cross-refer and to draw attention to the whole of which these are parts.

Take the phenomenon mentioned above, the newcomer; although there are general concepts of the admission of a stranger, these have to be modified in all cases by factors like the time the group has been in existence, how cohesive it is, what kind of composition it has, the timing of the admission in relation to significant historical, current, and anticipated future events of the group, the qualities, experience, and expectations of both the group and its new member, and so on. The list is almost endless. There has to be a cut-off point beyond which such interlocking effects cannot be considered. Life is not long enough to work out even a small proportion of the influential patterns. But whether admitted into our calculations or not, they will still influence the life of the group and its members.

One way of looking at this in a relatively simple way is to consider the consequences of behaviour. A more interesting, but essentially more difficult exercise is to look at the 'unintended consequences'. This problem was, I think, admirably summed up by Katharine Whitehorn in her column in the *Observer* of 24 February 1985: 'Dipak Nandy's Law of Social Policy . . . that the most important effects of any social action are the ones which are unforeseen and unintended.' For the moment we will content ourselves with the former, though unintended consequences will also rate serious discussion later. However, the concept of 'consequence' used here owes little to that offered by Thorndyke (1931) in his Law of Effect, largely because, as will be discussed, consequences occur over a much wider range than that perceived by the instigator, whether satisfying or not.

Consequences

Perhaps one of the major problems of existence in any form of communal state could be described as 'consequences'. What follows as a predictable consequence of any piece of behaviour is only a very small part of what actually occurs. Thus when people become aware of the chain reaction or network of effects that has been set in train by an apparently trivial act, they are amazed. 'Whoever could have thought that all that reaction could have come from what I did?' or 'I never intended that what I did should have caused so much trouble' is the kind of common statement about such awareness.

These frequent disclaimers of responsibility are interesting for two reasons. Firstly, when the statement is being made, the area of effect is being seen in retrospect, which would seem to indicate that many actions are performed as an immediate response to the perception by the performer of the nature of the situation. When this kind of response becomes constant and unvarying, it tends to be regarded as pathological or at best habitual and otherwise markedly inconsiderate. Secondly, such a lack of awareness of the consequences of behaviour, while causing immense problems in personal relationships because of the 'hidden' nature of the sequence, causes even greater problems in organizational structures. This occurs largely because reasons other than the real ones are ascribed to reactions, and countervailing measures are taken based on assumptions that are not wholly or even partially founded on any objective reality.

Where the consequences of behaviour are the mainspring of the behaviour itself, then attention of a high order is given to what follows. But even then there seems to be some location of concern in either immediate or long-term consequences, but rarely in both together. Human beings do not appear to have much faith in their ability to predict outcomes, which should lead us to some consideration of why this is so. Is it because experience has inevitably taught us that prediction is at best unreliable and at worst devastatingly inaccurate?

It would appear that people learn to mistrust prediction, the assessment of consequences, and this may well be right. But the reasons why prediction appears not to work may have little to do with the concept of predictability and much to do with the act of prediction. Thus we may have formed poor habits of which the most common is perhaps to be prepared to found a prediction with a degree of precision on the basis of evidence the quality of which would in no way support such precision. Or perhaps the precise opposite is true; i.e. we found predictions of wide generality and cautiousness on evidence of an extremely specific and detailed nature.

Let us now try to gather together the implications of this, for talking about predictions would seem to indicate that one was pursuing a line of possible understanding which is as fallible as seeking to establish causes.

The consequences of behaviour are plainly visible, though as I have indicated the response may not be easily accepted because it may have been fuelled with energy and assumptions from other pre-existing situations. Predictability becomes possible when records show that a particular response occurs with a degree of frequency that would allow an expectation of the probability of its occurrence. Thus instead of the statement, 'When you do this, that occurs', to which the response could justifiably be, 'Not always', implying that the causal link is not inevitably true, a statement could be made along lines of, 'When you do this, the chances are seven out of ten that that follows.' This could then be followed by a question as to whether that kind of frequency is desirable or required. Prediction in this sense is a fairly accurate estimate of the probability of a consequence or consequences.

From a staff point of view this becomes a crucial assessment of the validity of any particular intervention; i.e. has it been shown to produce the desired effect with a higher-than-chance probability?

In working with groups, because the responses of group members may well be powered as suggested above, only by becoming aware of the consequences of those responses, by pointing them out and working backwards from that point, is there any chance of the hidden energy source being exposed. Until that happens or it is discharged elsewhere, little can be done about mitigating its effects.

The study of consequences is the only counter to the generally held idea that each social situation is unique. It may be different without doubt but it is not unique. Conversely, it is also a balance for the dictum that 'it worked last time let's try it again'. What should emerge is a careful analysis of situations in the light of the ongoing and repetitive nature of most of them and the production of responses based on that analysis designed to maximize the benefits for all concerned. 'In nature there are neither rewards nor punishments; there are only consequences' (Ingersil, quoted by Dr D. M. Bowker, letter to the *Guardian*, 11 January 1984).

NOTE

1 Discussions of the definition of 'group' abound. The article quoted here – DeLamater 1974 – provides good material. See also Shaw 1974.

2 Members

'Historically one of the main arguments for the study of groups has been that groups are not mere summations of individuals but a different system level, with properties arising from the pattern of member characteristics in interaction with the situation.'

(McGrath and Altman 1966: 60)

Any group is composed of its members: trite and obvious, but so often forgotten in the desire to see a group, any group, as an entity existing in its own right, that the point needs constantly to be reiterated. This has been carried to such lengths in the past that the concept of a 'group consciousness' has been postulated as something that had an independent existence, being somehow distinct from the consciousness of the individual members. Individuals can of course share their perceptions and thus increase the stock of what is available for all, and also the resources of a group are greater than those usually available to an individual, but no such thing as a group mind can be said to exist.

What is being observed in a group is a series of individuals who are responding to the presence of others and committing something of themselves − their experience, knowledge, emotion, etc. − to the group for the benefit of all. What can emerge is sometimes different and sometimes greater or lesser than could have emerged from a scan of the nature and abilities of the members. This is not to say that the group is something special; but the peculiar relationship of the individuals comprising it over the time of its existence elicits endeavour, response, and behaviour that probably could not have been brought out except in this particular combination, at this particular time, and in this particular way.

Members of a group bring to it the energy and potential resources that the group may eventually use in its lifetime. But it is necessary to allow for the fact that the group itself becomes part of its members' experience as they continue to attend. Each group is unique despite its apparent similarity to other groups and despite the fact that the dynamics of all groups are essentially the same, though varying greatly in amount, intensity, duration, and importance. Thus when group-behaviour literature presents the idea of shared experience as the distinguishing feature common to all members of any given group, it is referring to a unique experience of those members present. However, unless that experience is made explicit by each member present to the others present, it may remain largely individual-unique rather than group-unique; and only the latter generates a genuine sense of belonging.

This highlights the ever present dilemma of membership, which can be stated as, 'How much commitment or how much surrender?' Some religious organizations demand an almost total submergence of the individual in the groups that form the cells of the organization. Other group memberships are adequately maintained by a minimum investment of time and effort. In most groups, which are not at these extremes, there is a constant struggle for all members about how much of themselves they feel they can or should commit to a group experience at any time. It is axiomatic that such commitment bears a strong direct relationship to the individual member's perception of the costs and rewards involved mainly for him- or herself, but also and perhaps increasingly for the group as a whole.

It is just this fact that makes the groupworker's ability to hold the members of a group together essential, so that they can begin to make a realistic analysis of the cost/reward factors involved in continuing membership. For the benefits of so doing are by no means as obvious to some members of a group as to some groupworkers.

THE CONCEPT OF MEMBERSHIP

One of the fundamental needs of all human beings is for affiliation to others. Much evidence from social psychology tends to show that this need is more important to well-being than is often commonly held. For instance, it is held to be unchallengeable that affiliation promotes interaction with others, which in turn allows the monitoring of the responses evoked, so that it becomes possible to discover how we as individuals are regarded and to come to form a picture of the kind of person we are. There are other ways in which affirmation of the self can take place, but it is indisputable that without constant feedback from others we are wholly dependent for our self-image on the picture we have formed from previous responses. This is adequate for some form of survival, but enforced social isolation has always been a major punishment for wrongdoers, and experimental social isolation reveals that some very important nurturant has been removed from the isolate's existence with consequent personal deterioration.

New social situations are often fraught with anxiety precisely because we do not know experientially what the nature of the strangers (to us) will be. We are no longer sure whether they will see what we have come to believe others see us to be – which may be significantly different in different situations, but all having the comfort of familiarity – or whether they will see what we believe to exist but would rather others did not know about. We may even wonder whether they will see aspects of our personality that we ourselves do not even know about, which we may have had odd hints of the existence of from others in the past.

If choice is possible, we normally tend to select groups to join that we think will confirm us as being as close as possible to what we believe ourselves to be. We may accept something less than satisfaction in this area if we are compensated by satisfactions in others, but if the cost becomes too high we will leave. Thus membership of groups is ordinarily an affirmatory and confirmatory process that increases our satisfactions by meeting some relatively deep needs.

But not all groups are voluntary, nor is choice always available. We are born into a group that allows no choice of membership and, because of its nature, can exert extreme pressure in the early stages of our lives. The family probably sets the basic patterns of our response to group membership, which may be modified by later experience and by the intelligent application of learning, but will most likely never be wholly changed. Not all groups are founded on their members' need to belong; some are compulsory, there being no alternatives; whatever the reason, when membership is not chosen our ideas about 'groupness', about belonging, have to be modified.

One factor must be presented immediately. The membership of some groups, where that membership is not a voluntary act, is not based upon an affirmative need but upon dependence. Thus the members of a group may need each other in order to survive, to achieve, to overcome difficulties, to support, or to defend themselves. The co-operation that can exist in such groups may be of a very high order indeed, but it tends to be so only as long as the need met by the group continues to exist, or at least is thought to do so. Unless some other bond comes into existence during the course of meeting the original need, when that need ceases the group will disintegrate even if its members are still compelled by circumstances to continue to exist in close physical proximity to each other. So although we are going to concentrate on the characteristics of group members, it must never be forgotten that because an individual is present in a group it does not necessarily clearly define the nature of his or her membership of it.

THE CHARACTERISTICS OF MEMBERS

'It should be obvious to even the most casual observer of group behaviour that the functioning of the group is affected by the kinds of individual who compose the group. A person's manner of behaving, his typical reactions to others and his skills and abilities determine not only his own behaviour pattern but also, to a major extent, the reaction of others to him as a member of the group.'

(Shaw 1974: 10)

Shaw goes on to say that the personal characteristics that the individual group member brings with him or her influence the way the group works and how it gets on with its job. He also notes another factor of personal characteristics affecting group behaviour as the peculiar combination and grouping that exists in any group: what could be called the balance of characteristics.

McGrath and Altman (1966) suggested that the real relationship between the capabilities and skills of group members and their performance in the group was neither as clear nor as simple as was commonly supposed. Much of the lack of clarity occurs when two measures of capability are compared, these being objective measures of capability and reports by members of the group and by other interested people on individual capability.

> 'Thus it may not be possible to predict the performance of a group as a group, from knowledge of individual abilities however measured. The differential relationship of member abilities to individual versus group performance[1] certainly highlights the old question of whether individuals *summate* to form a group or whether the characteristics of individual members combine in some non-additive but otherwise unknown way.'
>
> (McGrath and Altman 1966: 56)

The higher the abilities of group members the more they seem to produce better *member* performance but not necessarily better group performance. The ability of group members to assess each other's capability is not good (though with contact it tends to improve), except in respect of the prediction of leadership potential.

If abilities are not good predictors of group performance, evidence shows that some characteristics are able to promote change more effectively than others. However, a caution must be sounded here. Much of the research and writing available about member characteristics and their effects in group situations is founded on concepts of individuality that are essentially alien to an understanding of group processes. Thus to attempt to discuss how human beings are moulded by group forces, and how the individual behaviour they produce is socially conditioned, is at odds with a psychology that lists characteristics as if they were the absolute property of the individual rather than the historical and recent accumulations of social influence. Such influences are made manifest through the individual, but that is not the same as saying the characteristics *are* the individual.

Thus responses to sex, age, race, and experience and the attitudes group members display or do not display, but which inform their behaviour, are all products of society, the particular society or part of society from which they derived their training and that continues to support and nourish their ideas. They may have been subjected to more than one such societal influence or set of influences, and their responses and attitudes may consequently have had several formative pressures behind them, making understanding perhaps even more complex. This is particularly so as it is wholly possible for any individual to hold completely contrary attitudes about some specific area at one and the same time and even to be completely unaware of the dissonance.

In essence, then, looking at member characteristics is rather like looking at the labels in a store; it gives some idea of what is there, but until we have sampled the goods and related that experience to our accumulated knowledge we will not truly understand or appreciate what is on offer. A label is only someone else's idea of how something should be described, and his or her priorities and assumptions of what is essential are not necessarily ours. Generalities about the characteristics of human beings are just that; general indications. For instance, we shall see that the older people get the more contacts they make and the more selective they become, up to the point where social mobility decreases and the process reverses. Individual old people, because of personality factors, experience, opportunity or lack of it, habit, and so on, may behave in very idiosyncratic ways. This kind of observation of differences of response can help us differentiate significantly unique formative circumstances from those more usually experienced, and thus assist our understanding of the currently displayed behaviour.

Alternatively certain personality factors and behavioural patterns produce higher rates of successful group outcome in given circumstances. This kind of cause/effect sequence is much more pragmatic and of much greater use to the practising groupworker than the generalized knowledge noted above. To know what characteristics a group has need of to enable it to get on with its work successfully, and to know where within the group or elsewhere those characteristics are available, leaves a groupworker with only the task of deciding by what route, in the light of his or her knowledge about those involved, he or she will attempt to bring the two together.

Mitchell (1975: 414), studying the effect of personal characteristics on individual behaviour-change in sensitivity groups, discovered that the most promotive factors were a high degree of:

(1) responsibility (perseverance, reliability);
(2) achievement (need to be successful to do a difficult job well);
(3) vigour (investment of energy);
(4) original thinking (flexibility and enjoyment of challenging tasks);

and to a lesser extent:

(5) dominance (need to control and be a leader);
(6) endurance (need to work hard at a task until it is finished).

Hindering the promotion of behaviour-change were:

(1) nurturance (the need to help others);
(2) succorance (the need to have help and understanding from others);

and to a lesser extent:

(3) autonomy (the need to be independent of others and unconcerned with what they may think);
(4) cautiousness (impulse control).

Mitchell has highlighted a very simple fact of group life, which is that for given tasks, in his case positive personal change, certain characteristics are much more likely to produce the desired effect than others, while some personal characteristics are a definite block to success. This effect can also be traced in our discussion later of status, roles, and influence (see Chapter 3), of decision-making (Chapter 4), and of leadership (Chapter 5).

Surveys of the research on the effect that the abilities of members have on group performance also show some interesting and almost unexpected results. Abilities of individuals are in fact not good predictors of group performance, though relevant job experience is; good intelligence and potential in members do not necessarily correlate highly with effective group performance. Nor are personality and attitudes consistently related to effective group functioning, though the fact that some extreme forms of personality are not found in a given group does tend to enhance that group's effectiveness.

The evidence is clear enough. Any group will use the resources that the individual members bring to it only if it can create a situation in which those resources can be freed for use, i.e. where the members feel able to offer them and where they can be used effectively when freed. Most of the research findings about personal characteristics and group performance were based on groups in which no special effort was made to attempt to free the resources available. What we do not know is what level of resource use is possible if efforts are made. Nor do we know which methods of attempting to free different combinations of personal resources give the best results. There is always the possibility that what frees some may well inhibit others.

Sex

In considering the basic processes of interaction in small groups, Argyle (1969) reviewed some of the available research about the behaviour of the sexes in groups. He found evidence on conformity, sub-group formation, and competitiveness.

(1) Conformity: where there is little interaction in a group, females tend to be conformers. But this is not the whole

story. When the perception of the group is that the tasks they are performing are regarded as 'male' tasks, or when they are regarded as 'judgemental', then the female group members are reported as being highly conforming. However, should the group task be seen as 'sex free' or 'feminine' by the cultural norms of the group, then female members are not conforming.

(2) Sub-group formation: the general trend, as Argyle puts it, is 'that females are more affiliative, more concerned with socio-emotional problems and less competitive than males' (1969: 238).

(3) Competitiveness: male group members attempt to achieve maximum personal gain; females do not, they try to achieve fairness and justice and to avoid competition.

In essence, Argyle says, males are 'exploitative' and females 'accommodative'.

I would suggest that, although interesting, such research findings are far too general to be of much value to the residential worker. What they show is that people operate in groups in ways that are derived from their immediate culture and experience. The same stereotypes, the same expectations of role performance as the group members have operated with all of their lives, are what is originally demonstrated when they operate in groups. During the course of the group, new attitudes and new insights into sexual roles may develop, but even then there is the whole problem of transfer of learning (see p. 200), from the enclosed system of the group to the larger society.

Thus group members of different age groups, coming from different cultural backgrounds, from subcultures within the larger culture, will have formed acceptable attitudes towards sex roles and be imbued with the traditions regarding the behaviour to be expected from members of each sex. Apart from the driving force of sexuality – and even this has culturally defined behavioural manifestations – sex roles are based on conditioning processes similar to the formation of other attitudes.

Sex difference may well serve as a focus for all those group behaviours that come with the perception of difference, e.g. status, liking and disliking, power, scapegoating, and sub-group formation. But to round off this brief look at the possible effects of the sex of group members we must look at one piece of research into the effect on the leadership role.

Various researchers – Mills (1964), Hackney (1974), and Wright (1976) – have attempted to assess the effect of the sex of the group leader on the group.

> 'Gender of authority figures also has a clear impact on the behaviour and feelings of those who are subject to this authority. Specifically, women in authority generate more extreme reactions than males in authority, and, again, female subjects tend to be more extreme in their response to female authority figures.'
>
> (Wright 1976: 434)

Wright's findings tell us a great deal about the society in which they were conducted, in this case the student population of three New York City colleges. But some of his other findings have a measure of interest in the study of group leadership. He discovered that response to leadership style was relatively marked in the group members. Leaders who were open, friendly, and responsive to group members created amongst these people a high positive rating for each other; conversely when the leaders were distant and only coldly responsive, the ratings members had for each other became negative. Where both leader and group were female, the negative response generated by a distant leader became extremely marked.

Once more it would not be safe to generalize from these findings too much. Yet they do serve as indicators, particularly of the sex-linked nature of some of the responses to authority figures.

Age

> 'The fact that persons of different ages behave differently is no secret; children do not act like adults, although some adults behave like children.'
>
> (Shaw 1974: 10)

There is no doubt that age differentiates behaviour. Children start with a few social contacts that are essential to their well-being, which can, because of this essential nature, exert an enormous effect upon their behaviour. As they grow older the number of contacts usually increases dramatically, and the relative importance of any one tends to fluctuate with the availability of appropriate alternatives. Late in life – or sometimes earlier due to illness, disability, or other limiting circumstance – the number of contacts may diminish rapidly and the degree of stimulation they afford likewise.

Increasing age brings with it the possibility of cumulative experience, which generates a perspective of current events. Young people have no such backing from experience and are usually resistant to some degree to seeing the experience of others as being relevant to their perception of their situation.

Shaw (1974) summarizing what little research existed about the effects of age on group behaviour, noted the following.

(1) The relationship between age and group conformity is related also to the kind of pressure that is being exerted. Thus if the pressure is seen as coming from the peer group, younger members show increasing conformity and older people decreasing conformity; if the pressure is perceived as being exercised by authority figures, then conformity is highest amongst the lower age group.

(2) There is no clear relationship between leadership behaviour and age, though there is a slight tendency for effective leaders to be older than their followers, presumably on the basis of greater experience. However, the rate at which experience is acquired and assimilated may make significant holes in this hypothesis if in any one group vastly different rates of exposure were found.

(3) Older people tend to be more selective in the type of contact they make, which may pose some problems when groups of individuals are brought together by forces that to a large extent ignore the element of personal choice.

'To the extent that age is related to behaviour in groups, it provides an opportunity for the individual to learn appropriate social responses. It is not the mere fact that the individual has aged that is important, but rather that he has had greater experience in social situations.'

(Shaw 1974: 10)

Klein (1972: 64) assumed that age in adult groups was not a very important variable, but he gave the following examples where it would be important:

(1) Sixty-fives and upwards.
(2) Young married groups.
(3) Premarital counselling groups.
(4) Young adult groups.
(5) Groups for parents of disturbed children.

What emerges from this classification is that the age itself is not all that relevant, but an interest that is age-related is. Thus in establishments containing wide age ranges like prisons, the social groupings that occur tend to be based, apart from on opportunity, on compatibility of interest, which is often though not always age-related.

As we shall see with the factor of friendship, similarity is a major 'combining' feature:

'groups of people of the same age "have an inherent tendency to solidarity" because they share the same emotional strains and experiences in growing through a period of transition and are at the same place in life in facing their destiny.'

(Hartford 1971: 100–01, quoting Eisenstadt 1964)

Being in the 'same place in life' usually means being roughly in the same age group, but it must be remembered that the similarity is the binding factor and not the age group.

Experiments with residential groups constructed on the basis of an extended family have shown that in this context people with wide disparities in age develop an ability to relate, to support, and inform each other. What really happens is that, when successful, such a group is able to exploit all the different resources of experience, knowledge, energy, skill, and affection that are available to it.

Too often age difference is seen as an insuperable barrier in the same way that cultural and racial differences are. The fear of difference is very strong, and the pull of familiarity often stronger still. As far as group behaviour is concerned, different age groups have got different contributions to make and they have different requirements and needs that the group can meet.

Race

'Certainly blacks, like women, have been constructed as possessing the characteristics which are negatively valued in white culture, for example emotionality, sexuality and hedonism. The valued norm remains white, blacks being evaluated according to their distance from it.'

(Henriques *et al*. 1984: 89)

There appears to be very little material in groupwork literature and research that is specifically concerned with the effects people of different ethnic origins might have upon any group in which they are members. The discussion, as far as it has been noted, revolves upon three central issues: (1) the kind of group-work that may be used to assist people of different ethnic back-ground with the problems of living in a 'host' community; (2) the very important aspect of what effects within a group may be directly related to its having a mixed racial composition; and (3) how different races respond to being members of groups composed of monoracial members.

The first issue (1) produces material that is not markedly different to what is available about groups with disadvantaged people in society in general. Thus the evidence is related to (a) experience of poverty and social disorganization and (b) a background of common daily living experiences and feelings of worthlessness and inadequacy.

Beck, Buttenwieser, and Grunebaum (1968) discovered that the groupworkers, in this case therapists, working with 'lower class parents', comprised largely of ethnic minorities, were privileged 'to remain silent and learn about them without intruding their ignorance and differing value systems into the therapeutic process'; while the group members, i.e. the parents, were able to function as a resource sharing group.

McArdle and Young (1970) found that mixed groups of white and black students had expectations of each other that reflected the general ideas of their communities – ideas that, had they operated as hidden agendas, would have made working together very difficult. For instance, the white students expressed fear of the black students as a group; they were surprised that the black students wanted to preserve their culture and style and did not favour assimilation.

Levinson and Jensen (1967) discovered that there was no difference in overall interaction between black and white therapy-group members, though black members talked more often when the group leader became assertive. Fewer 'natural' leaders emerged from the black groups whatever the leader did; there was no difference in the verbal hostility expressed in black or white groups; black group members expressed a preference for a group leader who was forceful.

Given that these reports date from a period of racial behaviour in the USA that has now changed considerably, they can be used only to indicate the general theme of difference, which is in no way wholly related to race as we have seen. Groups composed of people from different racial backgrounds only emphasize the differences that exist in any group of people but are masked in groups from the same ethnic background by the overall assumption of similarity. Working in groups, people tend to find the similarities easily enough, but the differences of attitudes, opinions, beliefs, understanding, and concern are unsuspected.

'Sensitivity and responsiveness to, and understanding of, the hopes, wishes, and predilections of many different people are prerequisites of effective practice.'

(Southwick and Thackeray 1969)

The natural concomitant of such sensitivity is to recognize that racially different group members bring with them different resources, different understandings, different experience. It is the positive factor of attempting to get such a group to transfer the skills and resources they already possess to the current situation that is most important. Racial difference is often very visible, however, and this visibility may draw down upon such group members the dislike of the rest of the group in the act of scapegoating (see p. 145); but the techniques and methods of coping with this phenomenon are well covered in the literature.

Experience

> 'The experiences of individuals in a through culture determine member behavior in groups.'
>
> (Zaleznik and Moment 1964: 57)

'Experience' is a very wide term, and there is little research to give a lead to what kind of experience is beneficial to group performance. Wide general experience of life in a given cultural setting and specific experiences are all available to group members; but while experience itself is one thing, the response to it, the learning, if any, that comes from it, and the way it operates to condition future behaviour are something else. Often enough we hear people criticize others on the basis that they, having had prior experience of a given situation, should know better how to cope with it than those with no such experience – ignoring entirely the quality of that experience.

What is available for consideration is as follows:

(1) Group members with training in the specific task with which the group is engaged perform better as individuals, as does the group to which they belong, than group members without such training.

(2) Likewise group and members perform better when the latter have had good experience of group membership and training.

(3) Experience is not related to group performance on a clear-cut 'the-more-the-better' principle, but on the basis of appropriateness for the task in hand, in quality as well as in quantity.

(4) Appropriate experience operates as what McGrath and Altman (1966) call a 'mobilizer' of individual and group productivity potential.

(5) Experience has a direct relationship with the group's ability to develop favourable interpersonal relationships, which in turn affects the group's ability to develop its potential.

Although these five 'facts' are well documented in groupwork literature and have the nature of accepted evidence, there is little hard understanding of the reasons that lie behind the effects. For example, what particular aspects of appropriate experience translate into behaviour patterns that enable a group to be more functionally effective? Is it just the 'it-worked-when-we-did-it-this-way-last-time' syndrome? Is it that certain basic principles emerge from appropriate experience?

Several possibilities have been put forward, usually related to the way appropriate experience may facilitate how a group handles information. Thus trained and experienced group members may:

(1) generate information required by the group much more readily;
(2) make its transmission more efficient;
(3) ensure that there is much less waste of resources both in the analysis of information and in its synthesis.

In short, appropriate experience may well have developed procedural patterns based upon a recognition of what is available and upon knowing the probable consequences of making choices. If we look at the consequences of previous 'poor' group experience, it should become clear that experience generates a set of expectations, in this case of possible hurt or uselessness (see p. 137).

Good expectations based on past good experience rest upon a knowledge of what can happen that may well be strong enough to resist an initial period of current bad experience. The problem is twofold. Firstly, the good experiences of the past have to be brought into the present; secondly, the bad experiences have to be recognized as such and their probable influence understood and allowed for.

At the risk of appearing to state the obvious, it must be reiterated that the sole basis of assessing any new situation is the way it compares with our experience of something relatively similar in the past. There is no 'clean-slate' approach, nor is there any possibility that the major consequential markings on the slate are clearly visible; they may not even be known to the individual. Nevertheless they are there.

This chapter started with a quotation suggesting that groups were not mere summations of individuals, but a new system created by the interaction of member characteristics and the situation. Experience is a fundamental member characteristic, not only in its own right, but also because it conditions what kind of perception the individual has of the situation. It is thus doubly important as a permanent and active personal and private agenda. Its influence can be exposed only when within the group each member is able to express some elements of this experience and share them with others.

Much group research shows that group members are not very good at assessing each other, especially in the early stages of a group's life. They are somewhat better at evaluating group leaders. Thus group members consistently assess poorly the experience of their peers in nature, quality, and quantity; this, allied to the idiosyncratic assessment of the value to the group of their own experience, poses quite a task for a group leader. He or she has to create a situation that, while secure (see p. 81), also generates sufficient behaviour on the part of the members for assessments of what can be produced and what is valuable to be made, and in essence to create a somewhat different basis for assessment than existed previously.

Attitudes

'we know very little about the impact of attitudes toward the task and the situation on member and group perform- ance, or on interpersonal relations in the group.'

(McGrath and Altman 1966: 57)

In the years since the above quote was written there has not been a great deal of change. Even when a specific variable like authoritarian attitudes has been studied both in members as a personality factor and with leaders deliberately introducing an experimental situation into groups, the evidence is still confusing. For instance, authoritarian attitudes inhibit perception by others of the possessor or purveyor of such attitudes as a friend or leader, but positively enhance relationships connected with achieving and striving for high status within the group.

One fact that emerges from the research is that members who have favourable attitudes towards the group and its business tend to be people who have high status in the group, are relatively free to choose the jobs they do, and operate in a co-operative group system. In other words, favourable attitudes are significantly related to personal success. However, these favourable attitudes show no correlation with the quality of the individual's performance in the group or with the quality of personal relationships within the group.

There is some evidence (Newcomb 1963 and 1965) that over a period of time a group which works together and is cohesive will modify the attitudes of its members so that they become more alike. The same research also showed that the attitudes of different groups which may be in conflict or competition grow further apart.

The difficulty of ascertaining the attitudes of group members or of anyone else for that matter, except in obvious and public areas, makes the task of discovering how they affect groups almost impossible. Yet one of the most common reasons offered for particular group behaviour is that the attitudes of at least some dominant members are responsible for it. The notorious emotional content of any attitude means that it is not particularly susceptible to logic, and attitude change within groups is largely accomplished by group members beginning to feel that their peers are worthwhile people and their opinions worthy of consideration. As we shall see, this may be a public conformity move that is related to increasing acceptance by the group and thus a bid for safety rather than a move towards whole-hearted acceptance of different attitudes.

Attitudes that have been generated towards group behaviour by past devastating group membership will raise grave problems about future group experience in exactly the opposite way that previous good experience may have generated sincere but perhaps unrealistic expectations of what groups can achieve. These simple facts are extraordinarily relevant to people whose migratory life compels them to be exposed to one new group after another. Set patterns of survival backed by strong and reinforced attitudes may well have formed, and will therefore emerge as response patterns to any new group experience.

MEMBERSHIP OF RESIDENTIAL GROUPS

Now we must translate the foregoing material into the group-living situation, bearing in mind all that has been said about the nature of group living (see p. 10).

Let us start with a reiteration of the need for caution noted in Chapter 1. Caution is necessary for several reasons. Firstly, there are cultural differences; secondly, there are time lags; and thirdly, attitudes and opinions change with much greater rapidity in our modern society than most people are prepared to accept.

The race issue has highlighted cultural factors that were already present but obscured until large numbers of immigrants arrived in Britain. The cultural patterns of people living in different areas of Britain and their methods of handling social situations have always been significantly different in emphasis at least. Few people knew about them or made allowances for them because it was generally accepted that, in a relatively small island with an overall national culture, the similarities were more important than the differences. Whether this was true or not is not the salient point. What is important is that whatever differences were seen to exist, instead of being a source of conflict and subject to attempts to belittle or to conformity pressures, should have been seen as 'richness in diversity'.

Any institution, however effectively run, must reduce the options for individual behaviour. Like society in general, accepting collective benefits implies some degree of curbing individual and idiosyncratic expression. Society is large enough in most instances to tolerate very wide disparities of behaviour without the central structure being threatened. The smaller the community the more constraining it tends to become, primarily because it is small and thus has less capacity to absorb difference and also because eccentric or deviant behaviour is much more visible. (This has some parallels with the effect of television on social behaviour in that selected areas have become almost instantly visible to all the rest of us, with some fairly drastic effects.)

Groups function effectively because under most circumstances they possess potentially greater resources than any individual. They also have in-built disadvantages in some aspects of creativity and of decision-making. Strangely, the factor that is potentially a group's greatest asset – its diversity of membership knowledge, skill, experience, and background – is initially, and sometimes terminally, also its greatest disadvantage. As we shall see, the task of freeing group members from their anxiety about difference, allowing them access to the resources of human experience supplied by their fellow members, and letting them share their resources with others is not easy.

Although the constraining factor of visibility in a group may inhibit the start of such a freeing process, conversely when that process has started, it and its consequences are also immediately visible and can be highlighted if necessary. If this process is seen as good and felt to be beneficial, then, because it is visible to all, the processes of emulation and of contagion can make its spread much more certain and rapid. This perhaps amounts to the fact that one of the major skills of group leadership is to be able to hold a group in existence long enough, and with sufficient rewards in continuing attendance, till the visibility of membership behaviour operates positively rather than inhibitively. Unless behaviour has become so habitually destructive that it is more powerful in its effect than the combined available resources of a group, then difference possesses potentially positive outcomes if given the appropriate space, time, and encouragement to develop.

The second and third reasons for caution are linked. Research into behaviour takes time to become public, and the changes in social behaviour come about fairly quickly. Not only does behaviour change but the attitudes also. Thus difference in age currently produces a greater discrepancy in attitude, not just to technological familiarity, but towards fundamental social behaviour patterns like work, sex, morals, and religion, than would have been common even twenty years ago.

Once more the fundamental concept of difference has to be explored; and once more the essential prerequisites of recognition that difference exists, and that the causes of that difference may be other than what they appear, have to be considered. Where the constraining factors of a residential setting conflict markedly with previous experience, then the differences become highly visible. For example, an elderly person who has lived a somewhat solitary but independent existence for a good number of years can show up as an obstinate and difficult resident when admitted to a residential group when fewer independent habits of thought and action form the basis of its existence. As we will see in Chapter 8, the admission of a newcomer to an established group causes a re-evaluation of existing relationships and can lead to rejection of the stranger if insufficient links between him or her and the group are established.

In a considerable amount of groupwork literature the concepts of 'difference' and 'dislike' are inextricably linked together, and both are bound to the idea of 'equilibrium'.

> 'States of equilibrium are characteristic not only of individuals, but also of groups of individuals . . . the individuals of whom a group is composed adjust their interaction rates to each other; as they separately attain equilibrium, the group attains it likewise. Therefore a disturbance which upsets the equilibrium of one member will affect the others also.'
>
> (Chapple and Coon 1965: 54)

Chapple and Coon believe that equilibrium within a group can be tested by two measures: (1) whether the rates of interaction between members are constant, and (2) whether the rates return to their previous level after a disturbance.

Equilibrium in this sense means a relatively static state rather than a flexible balance between different parts of a group. Thus if test (2) were found to be positive after the admission to the group of an independent elderly person, then we can assume that the equilibrium has been attained by integrating the newcomer by a process of absolute conformity (suppression, resignation, or survival adaptation). But equilibrium in the group could be established at a different level positively in terms of accepting the resources of the newcomer and adapting the group's functional level to take advantage of these resources and use them to the benefit of all, negatively by driving the group's functional balance downwards, by devoting energy to coping with the disturbing new element by suppressing it, or by encapsulating it. This second event produces a balance that has benefited no one, a kind of accepted and quiescent hostility.

This chapter has presented information about some of the characteristics of individual members of a group that have been shown to produce particular effects. Since recognition of the possible consequences of member characteristics is the first step in using them positively, although the information should be used with caution, it could be a help towards more constructive understanding in an area where confined circumstances make individual difference that much more noticeable.

NOTE

1 For a brief summary of the comparison of individual and group performance, see Douglas 1983: 77–82.

3 Group Structure

In considering groups, whose very nature is dynamic, the concept of 'structure' has to have a special connotation. It has to take on some of the dynamic nature of group life and in the process lose the rigidity generally accepted as the basis of structure and even some of the static and enduring relationships of part to part and of part to whole.

Thus we emerge with a definition of the structure of a group based upon the idea of 'frequency of occurrence', i.e. those behaviours, situations, responses, etc., of the members of the group that occur and recur often enough over a period of time to be both expected and predictable. Because the range of behaviours that can occur in group situations is relatively wide – although constrained by the individual's perception of what is or is not acceptable to his or her companions, and by how much he or she cares about it – then structures can form in relation to all major behavioural modes. In short, repeating patterns develop over time. Thus there are patterns of the roles that group members accept and perform; there are also patterns of the use of power, of communication, of energy, of leadership, of affection, of similarity, and so on. A good description of any group would include these patterns, their strength, the members who generate and maintain them, those who initiate change, and the time elements involved.

To be able to produce such a description requires two things: the ability to observe complex human interaction, and the patience to continue to observe over a long period of time for the patterns to become recognizable. The latter is a crucial point. A behaviour may be a unique response by a group to a given situation. No doubt it will contain within it many of the characteristics of the group's usual behaviour; it could hardly be otherwise. But as a marker of the structures existing within that group it may well be very misleading, and its 'unique' nature can emerge only when it is seen in the context of that group's behaviour over time. Uniqueness can be perceived only as 'difference' from an otherwise similar sequence of events.

From such pattern-recognition comes a level of understanding of how a group functions that involves knowing something of the complex of interacting systems and individuals producing the overall effect. This is important, because a given overall effect produced by a group can have been arrived at by a multitude of different constellations of possible components. It looks the same on the surface, but the constituents may be very different. A response based on the surface appearance with little knowledge of the chemistry that produced it stands little chance of success.

Thus if the group has been constituted to effect change, then some basic understanding of the structure that exists or is to be engendered is essential. In fact, the patterns that I have called 'structures' are some of the larger elements of a group which should be the focus of efforts towards change.

Residential institutions can be analysed or described in terms of the structures of which they are composed, an obvious case being the use of the power structure. Any structure that applies to the institution as a whole must of necessity rate differently with the sub-groups embedded within the organization. Thus the power structure existing within a closed prison may be officially determined by the prison system; but the way it is perceived may be entirely different in the two major sub-groups, the prisoners and the staff. An alternative power system is almost inevitable within the prisoners' group, which will be based upon different criteria to the official power hierarchy; within the confines of the possible, more respect will be given to this than to the formal structure.

Thus emerges one of the fundamental group facts of all residential situations: the split between the two major sub-groups, the carers and the cared for, the managers and the managed, the processors and the processed. The dichotomy is clear, and attempts to blur the distinction have never been wholly successful even when the two sides are the same people, as in self-help groups. Even where the ultimate decisions are made by the whole residential group, the distinction never disappears entirely. One group is there because it needs to be; another is there because it is working, doing a job however altruistically, however well incidental needs are being met. Inevitably the structure of a residential institution presents in some degree this dichotomous appearance. This is not to say that across that divide many bonds and bridges of affection are not built, but they are constructed in full recognition of the division, not as attempts to obliterate it.

One of the fundamental bases of a group is that it creates boundaries. The most important of these is the inclusion/exclusion factor. It is eminently easy to be a member of many groups at the same time, for membership is not wholly dependent upon presence. But it is possible to be physically present in only one group at an instant of time despite the fact that the group containing the individual member will be itself contained in a larger group and so on. So we are compelled to recognize that the structure of groups, while implying a binding together for their members, also generates a division in the exclusion of others who may belong to other groups but not to a particular group.

So while this chapter is almost exclusively devoted to the structure of groups, initially we have to look at how groups are composed – that is, at their constituent parts. There is a general belief that the composition of a group markedly affects the way it performs. Equally there is an idea that the qualities of the members are by no means an infallible indicator of the kind of group that will emerge when those members start to work together. Both general ideas are to some extent upheld by the research available to us.

GROUP COMPOSITION

'It is not the particular characteristics of an individual group member that are of interest here, but rather the relative characteristics of various persons who compose the group.'
(Shaw 1974: 16)

Group composition is the specific mix of people, personalities, characteristics, abilities, skill, knowledge, etc. that is found in a group at any period of time. If the members form the group in a wide sense, then their attributes are the group's resources in a rather more specific sense. As is nearly always the case, there are several ways of looking at this, but I think the two most straightforward ways will suffice here.

Firstly, there is the 'expectation' approach; i.e. given the fact that there is already a collection of individuals who are formed into a group, what can be expected in a realistic sense from that particular mix in terms of the job that they have been brought together to do? Secondly, there is the 'design' approach; i.e. if it is known that certain characteristics in combination produce known consequences, then a group can be created that possesses more of the required characteristics and fewer of other factors.

There are problems with either approach, most of which boil down to a lack of hard factual data. Other problems of a related nature lie in the sphere of the unknown. For instance, it is not possible to know with any degree of certainty what people are capable of, given certain circumstances so far unmet. The potential that people have may be hinted at in their past and current behaviour, but the extent, nature, and quality of what may be available is seldom known even when life-long surveillance has been possible. Thus the problem of isolating member characteristics and then noting how these characteristics function in various combinations and settings is a mammoth task. Little wonder that what we have after many years of research is a concentration of very few mixes – e.g. cohesiveness, compatibility, and degrees of similarity and dissimilarity – and some fairly general statements albeit useful ones, about the consequences of such amalgams.

Perhaps one of the most written about of these mixes is that referred to as cohesiveness, and this will serve as a prime example. Cohesiveness was defined by Festinger in 1950 as 'the resultant of all the forces acting on the members to remain in or leave the group'. In essence this means attempting to discover those factors in the group that the members find attractive or repelling – the balance between attraction and repulsion being the degree of cohesion within the group. This sounds simple enough until one begins to attempt to isolate and define the factors that rate as attractive or repellent to the individual members. Liking for other members comes high on this list, as does being liked; but this must be followed by every shade of preference, choice, and need, ranging through power, expertise, pride, success, esteem, and the whole gamut of human experience. So when we come to measure, it will be no surprise that the variables tend to be rather global, like personal attraction, communication patterns, and relationship to group performance.

The general factors that emerge about the cohesion effect in group composition are as follows:

(1) The degree of cohesiveness in a group affects a large number of group behaviours.
(2) Verbal interaction tends to be higher in cohesive groups.
(3) Cohesiveness is positively related to member satisfaction.
(4) Cohesive groups are more effective than low cohesive groups, but only in tasks that they find acceptable.

As long ago as 1969 Shalinsky was looking at the effects of group composition on social-work groups. Using a measure of compatibility evolved by Schutz (1959), he discovered that:

'groups of compatible individuals, as judged by Schutz's compatibility criteria, functioned consistently better than groups of incompatible individuals on four aspects of group functioning, interpersonal attraction, group attraction, co-operative behaviour and productivity.'

(Shalinsky 1969: 49)

Schutz's definition of compatibility was based on a relationship between people that 'leads to mutual satisfaction of interpersonal needs and to harmonious co-existence' (1959: 45). Once more we see research material significantly endorsing general and traditional wisdom. We have always known that a group of people whose needs and resources are complementary and interlocking have no need to spend energy defending or attacking when in each other's company. They therefore have more energy to spend on their joint aims, and it follows that they stand to achieve them significantly better than a similarly composed group whose members are defensive and mistrustful.

It is often said that harmonious groups are based on the similarities of the members; this, though true, needs clarification. Difference that promotes some conflict tends to keep a group alive, to provoke new ideas, and to generate the energy to try to put them into action. So the similarities of members should not be total; that usually leads to smugness, to looking inward, and eventually to a complacent stagnation. The similarities must be in basic variables, usually core factors that stabilize the group and give it a balance. This enables it to enjoy those differences existing amongst its members that, while exciting, do not essentially threaten the basic harmony. It is not possible to list these variables because in any group the core stability can be formed from many different combinations. Where such stability exists, a group can afford not only to accept but also to enhance most behaviour that will move the group towards achieving its goal. Whereas, where the process of uniting the group is still in large part or wholly to be achieved, differences have to be minimized, and firmly agreed routes to goal achievement are the first priority.

GROUP STRUCTURES

'The term "group structure" is usually used to refer to this pattern of relationships among the differentiated parts of the group. Although we usually talk about *the* group structure, it is important to note that this is a highly complex organisational pattern. Since the group can become differentiated along a variety of dimensions such as status, power, leadership, and so on, it is possible to conceive of several group structures.'

(Shaw 1974: 18)

As we shall continue to discover throughout this book, conceptual units and realities are embedded in larger units and contain within themselves smaller ones. In search of understanding it is absurd to isolate any unit from its context. Thus although it is possible to talk about the structure of a group, it is necessary to remember that the whole group is part of a larger structure and is itself composed of structures. In the same way that an individual may play a role within a small group, the whole group can play a role within the larger organization of which it is part. (See pp. 13 and 158 for example.) Therefore in this chapter we look at *structures* in the plural.

It is necessary not only to analyse the structures that may exist within a group, but also to realize that they are symptomatic of the way the group is functioning and, from the angle of intervention, that different kinds of structures produce different effects on the members of the group. For example, Berlin and Dies (1974: 462–71) attempted to discover what effects differently structured marathon groups had on socially isolated students. They found that the degree of structure present in a group was in itself a salient factor, the more structured group generating a safer milieu for the isolates by restricting the area the group would cover and thus increasing the predictability of the group experience. Glover and Chambers discovered that 'as structure is increased in small groups three of the four components of creativity – fluency, flexibility, and originality – decrease. Group structure does not seem to affect elaboration' (1978: 391).

These are two sides of the same coin; increased structure generates safety for isolates but decreases creative behaviour. In particular an authoritarian structure diminishes the creative response faster than any other structural form.

Another interesting fact about group structures is the response of group members to them. Although I can quote no research to prove the point, from my own experience I would assert that a group's preoccupation with the structures that exist within it demonstrates two very different interests according to when the preoccupation occurs. When a group has been newly convened, then for it to concentrate on structure is healthy because the group is trying to create precisely those patterns of behaviour that will meet its perceived needs at that time. Structure-creation is therefore creative and necessary. Equally, when a group is breaking up, a concentration on structure becomes once more necessary. In effect the group is taking to pieces what it built and has used during its lifetime. At various points in between beginning and end, events may occur that precipitate a review of the structure; but in the main with minor modifications it tends to survive intact. If the original building was very wrong indeed, then major change may be necessary, but the chances are that the group will not survive to make such changes.

When constant reference is made to structure and much time is devoted to such discussion in a group that has been in existence for some long time and that created its structural pattern some way back in its history, then experience teaches that the group is using structure as a 'safe area' of apparent work. Looked at from the other side of the same coin, it is a technique of avoiding the work the group knows it should be doing but, for some reason or other, finds too threatening and cannot admit to, perhaps from a sense that loss of esteem would inevitably follow. As discussion of structure is a seductive ploy, appearing on the surface to be rational and efficient, it is usually effective as a method of evasion. However, it is certain that little progress with the group's basic task will be made until either the reality of the need for a structural review is established or the source of the perceived threat is exposed and dealt with.

Where an 'open' system obtains, as in most residential settings, the structural patterns are often that much harder to identify for several reasons. Structures develop on the basis of experience; that is, when people interact they begin to form impressions of what they can do and of what others can do. Although some of the impressions are in existence before experiencing the company of members of a particular group — by reputation, hearsay, etc. — most are formed by the contact that takes place over time. Contact in this sense can be diluted by opportunity, numbers, change of personnel, and time itself.

Where a through-put system is in operation, and in particular where the length of stay within the system is short, the chances of getting to know others and of being known are diminished. Such systems often operate on a loose confederation of people with a fairly specific set of approved behaviours. Where some are short-stay and others long-stay then the system tends to be set by the long-stay members, who form a core group and transmit the culture of the group. The short-stay members accept or reject this culture as they choose, but they seldom modify it unless they are exceptional people or become long-stay residents themselves.

Large institutions offer the possibility of many more contacts than small ones, but large systems, because members can dilute the intensity of contact, tend to generate self-limiting contact groups within the system. Large groups allow people to hide, while small groups do not; small groups often intensify personal relationships for good or bad, while large groups offer frequent change to the dissatisfied, and so members tend not to work so hard at establishing satisfying relationships.

All these factors and others affect the structures within a group. Conversely a group that is perceived to have certain structures in one form or another is displaying in a clear way what its responses are to the situation in which it perceives itself to be. Either way the necessity of being able to understand the structures of a group emerges as of paramount importance, not just for those who are working with the group as an instrument of some beneficial endeavour, but even more for those who are members of the group and the ultimate beneficiaries of its functioning.

Status structure

Status is the ranking that members of a group confer upon each other. It tends to be based upon the perception of worth as conveyed by the world outside and also, more especially, based by the group members on their perception of the value of fellow members. The fact that status is given rather than being a trait of a member can be seen most clearly where an individual apparently possesses two different status levels in two parts of the same organization.

In a treatment unit for disturbed children, which while physically separate was organizationally part of a large psychiatric hospital, the regime was wholly group-oriented. The running of the unit was based upon parity of esteem for all members, staff and children alike, with a democratic discussion process used to decide upon all major issues. However, as far as the larger hospital was concerned, the members of the unit were still consultant psychiatrists, doctors, nurses, therapists, domestics, teachers, and patients and were accorded the status normally given to such people within the hospital system when any inter-action between hospital and unit occurred.

Although this example is cited to indicate the perceptual nature of status within a group, it could equally well be used to illustrate the effect of the hospital's attitudes as a constraint upon the unit. In effect the probability of being able to create a wholly democratic unit was badly diminished because it had been brought into being by an hierarchical system, the status system of the hospital; and the lack of such an hierarchical system in the unit could be seen as artificial. The results of this were that most of the children (and some staff) accepted the method of running the unit in this sense of artificiality, which meant they were playing a public-conformity/security game. At the same time, those who were trying to create the reality of the unit were constantly frustrated by the refusal of the others to accept as genuine the parameters they were trying to establish.

Status can be accorded generally or specifically; i.e. a person can be regarded as of high status because of the kind of individual he or she is, with his or her value accepted as being relatively constant, or the individual may be accorded high status for a period of time because he or she possesses attributes that are at that time of extreme worth to the group. When the situation changes, the individual's status is decreased. This squares very well with what French and Raven (1959) wrote about the concept of specialist power.

What actually is high status or more importantly how is status accorded to members of the group? Group research would suggest that those of high status: (1) are seen to possess skills highly relevant to the group task, and (2) more frequently produce particular kinds of behaviour, e.g. (a) attempt to analyse situations, (b) initiate action, (c) give information, and

(d) attempt to lead. Interestingly enough, people accorded high status seem to perceive themselves as being able to exercise authority, which they are able to delegate, and as being able to influence the behaviour of others. This is an indication of the way in which self-belief can be picked up by others. High-status members also: (e) show leadership behaviour in leaderless groups, (f) show greater involvement and higher task satisfaction, and (g) tend to perceive the group as going well. In general terms, status, while usually but not inevitably related to power, relates also to the group and to the motivation to group achievement.

The effect of status on group performance is not so clear. What evidence there is indicates that the connection is slight, though practice wisdom seems to accept that 'the more central a member's position in the group, either in the physical or functional sense, the greater would be his contribution' (McGrath and Altman 1966: 58) is close to truth.

Because status is accorded rather than being possessed, high status is inevitably also related to being liked within the group. In fact, personal attractiveness, high status, and attractiveness of the group seem to be a self-supporting cyclic system within the group, though this occurs more frequently in groups with an agreed goal or in ones that are transient than in groups with complex motivations. There also appears to be a direct connection between high status and leadership, which might be inferred from the behaviours associated with high status listed above. High status also has a direct relationship with the group's response to 'deviant' behaviour (see p. 94).

Role structure

It is not difficult to see social behaviour as the interaction of individuals all playing parts that are familiar, some of which are very consciously controlled and presented, others of which are habitual to the point that they are triggered without conscious effort. In any collection of people the performances produced will consist fundamentally of the habitual roles plus conscious additions that, while familiar to the performer, are drawn from a repertoire on the basis of his or her perception of what is appropriate.

This repertoire will include performances that either have shown some degree of success in the past or are all that the individual possesses or knows about. In the latter case a small repertoire will produce some very obvious 'bad-fit' performances. But this fact leaves open the possibility that people possess the ability to perform other different roles that are still compatible with their value systems, but which, for whatever reason, they have never had the opportunity to learn.

As far as group behaviour is concerned this poses some interesting possibilities. For instance, each group member will bring to the group a repertoire of roles that, whatever their quality and effectiveness may be, he or she has adopted as his or hers. During the course of the group's existence these roles will be displayed as they are elicited by the group's behaviour and by the individual's perception of their appropriateness as a response to it. Thus over a period of time it becomes possible to predict that given kinds of group situation will elicit specific response patterns from certain members, and the elements of a structure as previously defined will have been formed.

For instance, I have recently watched some thirty small groups of a roughly similar composition looking at the same given task. This task was not strange to them but was central to one of the major concerns of their lives. Left to their own devices as to how they should tackle the task, the range of possibilities open to them was wide. Significantly those groups that contained people with either good creative imaginations or more specific relevant experience, plus the ability to operate as initiators, produced the most exciting group responses. The quality of information in each group was not all that different, but the method of presentation was. In each successful group one or two people adopted leadership roles or the role of idea-generator, to the distinct advantage of their colleagues.

Analysis of group behaviour has revealed that some roles are effective in producing certain outcomes, others less so, and some are prohibiting. Situations can arise in which the group's known repertoire of roles is inadequate to move the group towards its goal. Benne and Sheats (1964) suggested that training in role performance was necessary in this situation to create roles that would be instrumental in meeting the needs of the group. Training would take up some of the available role capacity of members that was not being used. Benne and Sheats related the group's role needs to the stage of development of the group (see p. 67). Thus roles in terms of kind, combination, and balance would need to be produced appropriately.

'For example, a "young" group will probably require less of the role of "standard setter" than a more mature group. Too high a level of aspiration may frustrate a "young" group where a more mature group will be able to take the same level of aspiration in its stride.'

(1964: BEN-6A)[1]

It is customary in groupwork literature to define member roles in terms of their main effect. Although several kinds of category have been used they have much in common, thus: the roles that are related to the task that the group is currently performing; those related to maintaining the group in a functionally effective state; thirdly, roles that are individual in nature and related not so much to the group goals as to those personal goals of the member as a discrete individual.[2]

The more group members pursue their individual goals, the less effectively the group can pursue its aims, unless in some direct way the individual goals are contained within the goals of the group.

One further point should be made, which relates to sensitivity. The adaptability of the roles members perform if they are to be related to the group's needs at any particular stage needs someone in the group to be sensitive enough to those and to be able to express his or her perception. Structures emerge, as has been said, because of the frequency of occurrence of a behaviour over a period of time in response to the same or similar stimulus. Given that the response is a satisfying one, and that there are only a limited number of responses available, there is some danger that responses will be produced at inappropriate moments, because changes that have emerged have not been noticed. Thus a kind of stereotyping occurs in which a previously satisfying role is presented in response to a diminishingly accurate perception of a situation. This situation can usually be resolved by feedback drawing attention to the changed circumstances without confronting the role-player hurtfully, perhaps by suggesting the increase in satisfaction that could accompany a shift to a 'better-fit' response.

The role of group leader may be crucial in this situation both in being sensitive to the role requirements of the group, to the need to create 'better-fit' responses, and in introducing elements of learning about the essential benefit to the group of an efficient role structure. In much the same way that members bring skills, knowledge, and experience to the group they also bring the ability to perform certain roles. This ability has been acquired in the open market of social interaction and in most cases relatively haphazardly. There is usually little clear understanding of the consequences of the performances or why they occur, not of the difference in degree of the provoking stimulus.

Thus a relatively crude social instrument can be refined within the context of the group to be a much more effective resource with a concomitant increase in members' role repertoire and in the skill of appropriate use.

Communication structure

'Such attributes of the group as its manner of enforcing norms, the position of its individual members within the group, the individual's reference orientation toward the group, may all affect the nature of the communication.'

(Litvac 1967: 107)

Communication between group members is not necessarily or even most importantly verbal in character. But because verbal exchanges are easily seen it is upon the records of such talking to each other that researchers have based most of their data.

In their book on decision-making in groups, Collins and Guetzkow (1964) noted that communication between group members tended to stick to certain forms. Similar forms have been noted by other writers so they are worth looking at here. However, their main importance is that the data can be stood on its head as it were. For instance, Collins and Guetzkow say that people who initiate most communication tend to be high-status group members. Status is not always easy to adduce, but who introduces more communication than others is merely a matter of counting. Thus the more prolific initiators of communication may well be the group's high-status members on the basis of being more consistently involved with everything that is going on.

It is also relatively easy to see to whom communications are addressed. For instance, in a group where a member of accepted position within the group is showing a marked deviation in his or her opinions to the agreed opinions, then the level of communication addressed to him or her will substantially increase. This is logical. The deviating member is a worthwhile resource for the group and this justifies a large effort being made to convince him or her of the error of his or her ways.

One function of communication is to parade before the group the ideas, beliefs, opinions, and attitudes of the members. This demonstrates similarities and differences, abilities and attributes, so that the process of beginning to know what is what and where to fit in can be developed. The same system also demonstrates the power and influence some members can operate; it exposes the nature of members, and out of this exposure grow liking and disliking.

In essence the communication structure is so important because one of the main functions of a group is to define reality for its members, and this system is the main instrument of the definition. Groups tend to develop their own use of language, as witness the jargon of professional groups and the secret language of gangs. To a large extent language defines and restricts the concepts an individual can cope with and, perhaps more importantly, the way ideas, behaviour, and situations can be understood. Thus membership of a particular group may ensure that each member's perception is narrowed in certain areas, accompanied by a strong feeling of being confirmed as being correct in taking this viewpoint.

Communication structure is sometimes clearly defined not only in terms of who can communicate with whom, but also by the nature of the communication that may be made. Communication of important decisions may always be downwards from the high-status members to the lower. Ideas from the lower-status members may be difficult to get a hearing for and be treated with scant courtesy. The communication structure in these cases is almost identical with the power structure.

The intrusion from outside of communication to the group is often very revealing, especially where the outside authority uses a structure of communication that is essentially different to what exists within the group. For instance, a communication addressed to a group with a very dominant leader, and a power structure that requests an equal and democratic discussion of the information it contains, either requires that the group leader gives permission for this kind of response to take place or means that there is the possibility of a variety of different kinds of trouble. Control of a group most often resides in the person or sub-group in the centre of the communication network, who can monitor, interpret, transmit, or withhold as suits their purpose.

As we shall see (p. 183), feedback about the quality and nature of communication within a group tends to enhance it and also to develop a realistically based trust in its efficiency.

Warning must be reiterated about the form that communication takes. We live in a verbally oriented society and place a considerable emphasis on the efficacy of verbal communication. But words are often inadequate to express ideas, thoughts, and feelings, and often also counter-productive through possible misinterpretation. Any communication system within a group will develop a range of signals, gestures, and postures, the non-verbal clues that are particular to that group and can be truly understood only in the context of that group. Many such signals are universal to a culture, but many more become the copyrighted possessions of a given group, and this can develop into one of the many excluding factors with which groups create an identity and maintain it.

Leadership structure

As an entire chapter (Chapter 5) is devoted to leadership, and since it also recurs as a theme in many other places, we must concentrate here on the effect leadership has on group structure.

> 'Leader–follower relationships within the group may also be considered one aspect of group structure. . . . It is probably more accurate to consider *degrees* of leadership and follower-ship within the group.'
>
> (Shaw 1974: 25)

This statement indicates Shaw's belief that a leadership structure is based upon the amount, quality, and nature of the leadership acts found within a group, rather than on the relationship of master/disciple, which seem to be the image that most people have. In essence the leadership structure of a group is a refined version of its role structure. Given the fact that a group is not wholly dominated by an imposed or delegated leader whose position is legitimized and maintained by an impressive organization, and that group members have some element of choice, then leadership acts will be performed by those who can see that some such act needs to be made. It will also be necessary for the member so acting to believe that he or she possesses the necessary attributes to make the required try and also that it is worth the risk.

So within any group with some degree of member freedom the leadership structure will comprise the members who, believing they have something to contribute to the welfare of the group, specific or general, large or small, are willing to offer to do something. In this sense leadership acts are those behaviours that are made in an attempt to influence the total group's behaviour. Sometimes the structure that emerges is relatively clear. For example, one member of the group can always be relied upon to take over control when certain kinds of group problem arise. That member is operating in a clearly defined role, which has as its basic function moving the group at least away from point x, even if it does not also imply movement towards goal. That might be the function of another member.

The leadership structure must also contain people who do not initiate leadership acts but who actively support or oppose any that are made. Any leadership behaviour in a group is only as good as the support it receives. The structure must also contain those members who do not make leadership acts, nor support or oppose them. They may have learned from experience that nobody takes any notice of what they say, or they may be markedly indifferent to the outcome or even quite happy for any-one to do anything as long as it isn't them. Absence of comment in our society is regarded as tacit agreement, a collusive silence. It may not be anything of the sort, of course; it may be that the silent do not understand what is involved or do not have enough evidence to make a valid choice. I have often seen group leaders ask members to make choices in the total absence of any material that would make such a choice an intelligent operation.

A leadership structure does not have to be based upon the relationship of followers to an overall controlling leader. It may be a complex system of acts based upon individual perception of group need and ability.

The sub-group structure

Any large group will comprise a confederation of smaller groups whose interests are consonant with remaining in the larger group but whose aims are not necessarily wholly identical with those of the larger group. These sub-groups may be transient or perma-nent according to members' needs and the traditional practices of the group. The act of combination for peculiar advantage is perhaps one of the most common behavioural ploys that human beings use, and this is reflected in the number of terms that are available to describe such combinations. In the literature of group dynamics, 'combination', 'constellation', 'sub-group', 'clique', 'coalition', 'band', 'coterie', and 'gang' are only some of the many terms regularly used.

As I have said elsewhere (Douglas 1979: 189), the basic fac-tors serving to generate sub-groups may be listed as follows:

(1) Interaction.
(2) Common or similar interests, values, and attitudes.

(3) Physical proximity.
(4) Needs that complement each other and cause collusion.
(5) The presence of a focal individual or point of view.
(6) The need to resolve integration problems in a large group.
(7) Mutuality of feelings of attraction or repulsion.
(8) Pressure for minority representation.

Wilmer (1966) thought that psychotherapy groups were composed of 'free associations of people', which he categorized as (1) pairing, (2) cliques (usually of three members formed around one dominant individual whose behaviour or belief system is deviant from that of the group leader or the emerging group norms), and (3) free-forming small sub-groups based upon mutuality. Cliques tend to be unstable and to generate disorganization but may be useful as a discharge point for group aggression during periods of high tension.

It is from sub-group membership that security, affirmation, and acceptance come; it is also within sub-groups that challenge, disturbance, and moves to change the larger group and its processes are generated. A secure and powerful sub-group can bring about major shifts of direction, modify the group norms, emphasize and de-emphasize specific roles, and still remain within the overall ambit of the group.

Fisher (1974) asserted that sub-groups 'typically form and maintain themselves because of some conflict within the larger system'. Norton (1979) maintains that besides conflict the formative factors of coalitions are the popularity of an individual and mutual responses between individuals, which he calls 'reciprocation'. He also suggests that by noting and measuring the existence and intensity of popularity and reciprocation the sub-groups of any group may be assessed, with the identification of 'pivotal' members (linking two or more sub-groups by their multiple membership) and 'peripheral' members (attached but perhaps not involved).

Thus the general ideas about sub-groups link in with group ideas about security and safety (see p. 81), normative structures (p. 64), status (p. 51), and roles (p. 53), and illustrate once more the pointlessness of isolating one factor of the dynamics of a group and thus ignoring its interactive and embedded nature. But more specific ideas about sub-groups have come to be considered from the rather surprising angle of attempting to assess the number and nature of relationships that any individual can make. We are fully used to calculations saying that if a group comprises a given number of members then a very much larger number of relationships are available to them. But if we examine the quality of those relationships some are much more important than others, and in any case the factor that emerges most importantly concerns the amount of attention that can be given to relationships at an instant of time.

There are some theorists who maintain that the basic human group is the dyad (e.g. Smith 1978 gives a detailed analysis of the dyadic structure in groups). Others assert that, because the limitations of the interactive process are what they are, all groups are composed of isolates and pairs with linkages between them either permanent or transient, so that a loose constellation of pairs and individuals is formed with some common binding factors holding them in relationship to one another. If we now add to this the idea mentioned above of attention at an instant of time we begin to realize that sub-groups contain individuals who constantly pay more attention to their relationship with each other than they do to others.

Not that they are unaware of the presence of others, nor that they do not have relationships with them: but the amount of servicing they give them either suffices to maintain them in existence or allows them to lapse. The amount of servicing of hitherto neglected relationships will change dramatically with a change in perception of their value. Thus all sub-groups contain people with differing degrees of intensity of relationship, ranging from an almost totally committed one to those on the periphery, interested but only minimally participant.

It would seem possible that, at any moment in a group, any member may be in any one of several states regarding his or her sub-group membership. He or she may be:

(1) wholly involved in an interaction with one other member with an awareness of the presence of others and of yet

others not members of this particular group, they being almost background to the interaction taking place;

(2) not directly involved as an active participant in an inter-action but aware of the others of his or her sub-group, listening, maybe gesturing assent, but also aware of the presence of others and of the factors extraneous to the group as a whole; the individual may have a coolly observed idea of where he or she and others see the sub-group placed in relation to the group as a whole;

(3) peripherally interested in the sub-group's behaviour and his or her part in it but almost as equally interested in other sub-groups and individuals and his or her own part in relation to them and to the overall group;

(4) very tenuously attached for a moment because the sub-group seems temporarily to represent his or her interests, but the individual will abandon that attachment for another as soon as its value ceases to exist;

(5) not attached to any sub-group.

It may be noted that (4) and (5) represent different degrees of the other basic role, that of the isolate. But some group members also appear to operate as isolates in all situations, sometimes desperate, but are often relatively valuable and valued members; whereas others are isolates only transiently as they pass from one attachment to another. Group sociograms often identify such members as isolates where in truth they are 'birds of passage', as observation over a longer period of time would show.

As this chapter concerns group structures, and since sub-group formation is one of the best examples of such structures, it is perhaps appropriate to reiterate the basic facts of group structures here. Literally they are patterns of behaviour that repeat with a frequency and similarity permitting a relatively accurate prediction of their occurrence. Thus it is essential to know whether a transient attachment is an intermediate stage between two or more permanent attachments or part of a pattern of behaviour exemplified by being in a continual state of change.

NORMATIVE STRUCTURE

> 'The norms of a group . . . represent the expectations, aspirations, and hopes of the group as well as the recognition of the group's limitations. Group norms could be more properly thought of as a set of rules and standards rather than of observed averages.'

> (Bonney 1974: 448)

Bonney goes on to add the concepts of reward and punishment when behaviour exceeds the allowable limits. So in essence the normative structure of a group comprises a pattern of behaviours that are acceptable. At the outside will be behaviours that may bring either rewards or punishments because they are different; whether they are seen as good or bad will depend upon whether the group sees them as conferring benefit or not in terms of its current position.

It must be remembered that complete adherence to a set of rules of behaviour may produce stability, but it also inhibits change. As long as the situation in which the group exists is also equally stable, then its own stability may be an asset, though even here change could be sought. Where changing patterns in society are the rule, then stability within the group means getting out of step. This, of course, may be the very aim of the group but it can produce anomalies.

Consider the current employment situation. Preparation for entry or re-entry to work has long been a feature of a large number of residential institutions, but work is no longer readily available. If the programme of residential institutions' training is still work-oriented the gap between the training and the reality will be bound to cause problems. The work orientation may well produce stability within the residential group, but such a normative structure is no longer compatible with the norms of the larger society.

Williams, Martin, and Gray (1975) disputed the idea that norms are set up in a group as a result of interpersonal influence and that they remain part of the behaviour patterns even when the individual leaves the group in which they were formed. Collective self-interest may be a reason for forming acceptable patterns of behaviour, in which case it would be expected that when an individual left the group his or her behaviour would revert to previously held levels. Williams, Martin, and Gray discovered support for the idea that social norms 'take longer to extinguish than to form' but need not become a permanent part of an individual's personality.

A point of difference here may be how much the normative behaviour of a group accords with the previous normative behaviour of the individual, a situation discussed elsewhere in terms of public conformity and private acceptance (see p. 97).

Norms develop originally out of the patterns of behaviour that the individuals bring with them to the group. Where a group is already well established the newcomer may have the problem of integrating into it until two things happen (see p. 187). Firstly he or she learns and accepts within a given level of tolerance the norms of the group, and secondly the group becomes satisfied that he or she is tolerant of and receptive to these norms.

Acceptance of group norms brings benefits in many directions, not least in the element of security, the lessening of risk, and the encouragement of interpersonal co-operation. A normative structure creates a frame of reference for behaviour and indicates clearly what personal goals can be achieved within the group. In communication between members the normative structure establishes standard meanings for language and other group events, thus creating exclusive and inclusive factors and setting certain kinds of communication pattern to which members will pay more attention than usual.

The security element is backed by sanctions applied against non-conforming behaviour (see p. 97), which in turn increases the ability of members to predict. Though group norms are intolerant of those behaviours that threaten group security, they may be elastic for non-threatening behaviour, especially if it brings about beneficial change or is initiated by persons of high group status (see p. 51). Indeed, it is usually these high-status members who are the greatest influence in deciding what norms the group will adopt.

Even groups left completely on their own will develop norms, usually those that create a comfortable and untaxing environment. They usually cover only those aspects maintaining the group in existence.

For those who deviate from the group norms there are several possible options: to accept the norms and conform, to attempt to change the norms in their favour, to remain and accept a deviant role, or to leave. Problems occur where the deviate cannot leave, cannot change the norms, and is not able to accept those that exist. In place of physical withdrawal, psychological withdrawal may take place, which manifests itself as apathy or sickness but can also show as rage and violent behaviour.

It is interesting to watch newly created groups develop a system of rules of behaviour. Almost always most group members are wholly unaware that behaviour is being constrained until the opportunity to consider what rules the group is operating is given. As the task of the group is made more explicit, then rules can be formulated that facilitate its achievement; these are usually in addition to the formal or acceptable behaviour already in force. This process serves to refine the group by enhancing task-oriented behaviour and by degrading or diminishing non-relevant behaviours. The group is then moving towards a functioning unit governed by its own procedural rules, which are essentially adaptive.

So far two kinds of norm have been described as essential parts of the rule structure, but there is a third. These norms are usually described as informal, non-explicit, and general. They are rules of behaviour that may derive from the larger society or not; but when people are asked to describe the kind of behaviour that they regulate, phrases like 'what everyone knows is right' are used.

We must also consider the interlocking and interacting nature of norms. As we have seen and will explore further (pp. 158–62) all groups tend to be part of a larger group. Thus it is feasible that within any groups several normative structures may exist at the same time. The usual pattern is that where sanctions are effective or acceptance greatest this tends to make a normative boundary. Within it, all sub-groups conform within the acceptable level of tolerance to the norms of that group. Sub-group norms that are thus in no form of conflict with the large containing group norms, even if of a different nature, are of little consequence except in so far as they may be a source of the production of new and ultimately acceptable ideas. Sub-group norms that would be in conflict are thus necessarily secret and hidden. If they are not, then the sub-group has the choices open to it listed earlier as available to the individual deviate. Public conformity is the only real possibility for the sub-group wishing to stay within the confines of the larger group when its norms are essentially in conflict with those of the larger group.

There is no doubt, however, that where such a publicly conforming response exists the efficiency of the larger group may be impaired by the reduction of commitment to the group to a level that will ensure a tolerable level of safety. This situation is explicitly summed up by the phrase 'paying lip-service'.

FORMATION AND DEVELOPMENT

It may seem like putting the horse behind the cart to discuss the ideas of group formation and development after the material about structure. In one sense this is true but in another it is not. The thesis about the way groups form and develop is facile and easily grasped and is apt to make all the hard work needed to understand group structure apparently unnecessary. But the whole process of development is based on the interaction of the structural parts and so it comes here at the end of this chapter rather than at the beginning.

> 'Groups that maintain themselves through time, whether or not they are served by a practitioner, develop definite structures and deal with similar problems. They pass through roughly comparable stages and may develop roughly comparable patterns of organisation.'
>
> (Glasser, Sarri, and Vinter 1974: 32)

Groups form in the same kind of way that water condenses out of air, i.e. from a huge mass of isolate particles when the conditions surrounding them are right a grouping together of a number of particles occurs; they then stay together and form a significantly different entity. The major difference between water-drops and groups is that the former having condensed into a liquid form, contain the particles of which they are composed in the one combination. By contrast human beings spend some time in several combinations over the same short period of time.

Group behaviour is elicited by the presence of others, but in all but a very vague sense of the word a group does not 'form' until its members have some shared experience – in other words until they become aware that being with these selected other people provides a unique experience that enables them to identify the boundaries of that particular group as a unit distinct from other groups in which they simultaneously hold membership. This identification as being part of an existing unit usually occurs when the group has gone through a round of dealing with the anxieties of members about their commitment to the group as against the attractiveness of other things and about the degree to which the group will influence their behaviour and present them with opportunities to be liked and to like.

Thus one of the 'stages' reported by Glasser, Sarri, and Vinter above is clearly a prerequisite to working as a unit; i.e. the unit has to be created, which takes time. Some groups never complete this unit-creation task, and some do it only partially. For instance, where a group exists by virtue of each member having a similar relationship with a central person, then the unit-nature of the group is created by that relationship being held in common and not by the discovery by each member of their belongingness acquired by an investment of energy and created over time by shared experience. The difference is subtly difficult to describe but fundamentally very marked in practice.

The development from the forming stage of any group depends upon refining the initial stage even further along the lines that increase the efficiency of the group in performing whatever function it was created to achieve. Many writers see these stages as following in linear sequence, i.e. each arriving out of the one before it in time. But this is essentially simplistic. Groups meet with set-backs in their development and are often compelled to go over the same ground several times. Outside factors may alter a precarious balance: change of environment, redefinition of purpose, changes of membership, leadership, renegotiation of rules of procedure, and so on. Smooth progression through a series of stages to run-down and termination is a theorist's ideal seldom met with in practice.

Many groups, particularly in residential settings, are not clearly defined in terms of beginning and end. They are largely groups open at both ends; new members are constantly seeking admission, and old members are departing. This would be expected to make modifications to the ideal concept of development as a series of stages and it does. Much practice evidence shows that to add or subtract a member creates a group different from the one that existed prior to the addition or subtraction. In fact it throws the group into the process of re-establishing an element of shared experience (see p. 187).

There is also the problem that open groups do not end in the sense that a closed group does when it has completed its task or when it is disbanded for other reasons. In an open group, members close their membership as individuals, which is essentially a different kind of parting to what occurs when all the members leave together. In open groups the group continues to exist and can still be visited (in theory if not in practice); closed groups that terminate are a memory for their members and have no substantial ongoing existence.

So development in a group is seldom smooth and in open groups in particular it is very hard to assess. This poses problems because groups at different stages of development can cope differently with the problems they face. Thus a group that has a constantly changing membership, even though its total membership is the same, has at each session to go through a fairly lengthy period of re-establishing its relationships (within the group) and also its identity. It can therefore never be expected to proceed to deal with anything more than minor facets of its actual business and must always be concerned with normative behaviour and with structural matters.

Much of the material on group development is readily available. The following series of comprehensive articles on the subject should enable the reader to fill out to his or her own satisfaction what has been presented here. See, for instance,

Hare 1973, Gibbard and Hartman 1973, Hill and Gruner 1973 (all three articles to be found in *Small Group Behaviour*), and Douglas 1970 (a summary of some of the major ideas).

THE STRUCTURE OF RESIDENTIAL GROUPS

What emerges clearly from this consideration of the structure of groups is that all the structures not only are interlinked, but appear to be different ways of looking at the same basic pieces of information. Take status, for instance. When a group member is accorded high status by his or her colleagues he or she will take on certain roles within the group; such a person will initiate and direct more lines and types of communication; he or she will be the centre of sub-group formation, will be largely instrumental in ensuring the kind and number of norms and standards that the group will adopt, and will greatly facilitate the group's development; in short, he or she will exercise a major influence over the total functioning of the group. It would seem a circular logic is at work here; e.g. a member is afforded high status within the group because he or she can demonstrate his or her worth; this member can then exert influence through all or most of the group structures. Because in doing this he or she is seen as a person with power and influence exercised for the group good, the individual is accorded high status!

The basic pieces of information must therefore be concerned with the ways in which individuals behave that attract to them firstly the acceptance by others of those group roles containing the power to influence others, secondly the submission of others to the exercise of that power, and thirdly the according of status and position that legitimize the exercise of power. Thus within any group there are several focal people who are almost always the central point of one or more group structures. If it is a large group organization, these focal people may be co-operative – cohesive to a larger idea that unites their individual power points – or they may be in conflict with the objective of coercing each other to obtain a greater spread of influence.

In nearly all residential settings one of the two major sub-groups possesses legitimate power and expert power not available to the other, based in a system that not only maintains the difference in power but seeks to define and enhance it on the assumption that it is necessary to develop an efficient system. Therefore all such systems show a marked formal distribution of power; the powerful sub-group maintains major control over communication systems, over the rules of procedure, and over the positions and roles of the members of the less powerful sub-group. This latter is therefore less cohesive depending on the degree to which the individuals who comprise it see that most satisfaction can come to them by accepting the role and status within the system as defined by the major sub-group. So it may appear to be more rewarding to be a member of Mr A.'s pastoral group, where Mr A. is a member of a powerful staff team, than to be a member of an informal residents' group dedicated to attempting to achieve some control over issues that centrally affect their lives.

In so far as people may be members of many groups simultaneously, though usually only physically present in one at a time, it is possible for individuals to act as members of a structure dominated and controlled by a powerful sub-group while remaining committed members of a group that is part of a different structural arrangement. Thus staff within a residential unit may well act within the norms of the formally accepted confines of their contractual obligations to the treatment process of the unit and yet actively pursue membership of a sub-group that almost totally rejects that process as invalid. While this may be a morally untenable and uncomfortable position it may also make excellent economic and promotional sense, especially in times of extreme unemployment.

The structures of any residential unit will be complex and not necessarily obvious. But it is certain that much of the behaviour which becomes obvious does not wholly rest in individual responses. To understand such a unit requires a knowledge of structures and of the standing of individuals and sub-groups in relation to them, and some recognition of those structures that are more or less permanent and those that are essentially transient, being dependent upon *a* person or *a* situation for their existence.

'A group is influential because it can define reality to a person through an infinite variety of sense data and by the definition which a group gives to those data experientially.'

(Klein 1972: 122)

NOTES

1   This text has an idiosyncratic method of page numbering; the paper by Benne and Sheats (1964) runs from BEN-1A to BEN-9A.
2   I have not given a list of roles available within the three major categories because most of them are well known from the literature. Those not familiar with these descriptions will find the necessary information in the following sources that I have used in this section: Benne and Sheats 1964; Golembiewski and Blumberg 1970: 86–90; and Klein 1972, chapter 3: 90–106.

4 Group Behaviour

Residential institutions of all kinds create a containment situation for their residents. This means that they form at least a clearly visible boundary, and events can be defined in that they occur within that boundary or outside of it. Seepage of influence across that boundary from the outside inwards and from the inside outwards may be great or virtually non-existent, but the boundary can be seen to exist.

Apart from being a physical boundary, the residential establishment is the place where a considerable amount of time is spent. Residents are brought into relational contact with other residents and staff on the basis of a much higher level of contact than would be the case in ordinary society outside, because the choice of contact is strictly limited by the numbers available or by the rules of procedure. Ironically there are isolates in our society for whom the contacts available within a residential establishment (e.g. a prison, where contacts are seldom at a high frequency level due to supervision difficulties with insufficient staff) are infinitely preferable to the almost total lack of contacts in the supposed freedom of society at large.

Thus one group factor that would seem relevant here is that of relating to role models; in the case of the following illustration, the model offered by the warden:

'Sinclair (1975) studied the quasi-family institutions of probation hostels and in particular the differential effect on the behaviour of residents of different warden/matron pairs. He found that the warden's performance had a profound effect on the residents, much more influential than that of other staff.'
(McCaughan 1980: 159)

This is wholly in accord with the received knowledge about group behaviour. Where people find themselves in an unfamiliar

situation they tend to follow the example of apparently acceptable patterns of behaviour of those who seem to know what
they are doing: 'when reality is unclear, other people become a
major source of information' (Aronson 1980: 26).

All the studies on conformity show that in uncertainty people
look for models to follow.[1] The supply of such models is never
unlimited; but in any group, and in particular any residential
group, the immediate availability of a model of acceptable
behaviour is even further reduced. The influence such role
models can have is very great indeed as much when it is negative
as when it is positive, when it is rejected as when it is accepted.

So residential establishments would seem to create a behavioural boundary by reducing choice of role models in the same
way that choice is reduced in other aspects of life, e.g. freedom.
Influential characters, i.e. those perceived as possessing high
status within the group, have a disproportionate effect within
the confines of a residential establishment. There are few
alternatives and their power is not diluted by being only one
among many.

Of all the behavioural patterns that can occur within a residential setting, violence tends to promote the most anxiety.
Even within the less restrictive bounds of a group outside the
residential scene, the onset of violent behaviour is regarded with
trepidation, and a very frequent question I am asked is how one
might deal with this. Usually there is little theoretical understanding of the causes and precipitating factors of violence and
seldom any techniques for handling it other than those learned
by hard experience. Not that the latter are to be disregarded;
they are often very effective, but they tend to have been developed to meet specific situations and are seldom directly trans-
ferable to others.

As with other behavioural responses when they occur within
the intensifying setting of the residential establishment, violence
tends to be qualitatively different. The small compass in which
it occurs, often the lack of restraining bonds of affection or
respect, and the effect of cumulative unexpressed anxiety,
anger, or frustration can all contribute to the appearance of a
major damaging explosion. In this chapter we will have a brief

look at violence in groups; we shall also consider the concept of safety, the process of decision-making in groups, the concept of territoriality, individual- and group-limiting behaviours, and finally deviance and conformity.

We will not be considering the patterns of behaviour in a general sense – much material is already available in that area – but rather the ideas there that might increase the understanding of these behaviours within the residential institution. Above all, we will try to derive some practical knowledge from this procedure.

> 'All behaviour is mentally controlled and the operation of psychological laws cannot be suspended by romantic conceptions of human behaviour, any more than indignant reaction to the law of gravity can stop people from falling.'
>
> (Bandura 1969)

VIOLENCE

> 'Violence is essentially wordless, and it can begin only where thought and rational communication have broken down.'
>
> (Merton 1948)

Whenever residential workers gather together, one topic of discussion is almost certain to be that of violent behaviour. Mostly this means the violent behaviour of the residents in their care, but occasionally it concerns the violence by which the staff respond to the frustrations and the often infuriating nature of their work. The discussion of stress, of anger, of control also assumes a large part in these conversations. Here is not the place to debate the many varied theories and ideas that have been put forward in attempts to explain violence and aggression; there is a massive literature on the subject for it is one of the most written-about themes in social science.

It is essential to remember that one major effect of being contained in a residential situation is that an individual is exposed to the presence of others, who are not present by his or her choice, far more than in most other living situations. Where choice exists then the level of exposure can be controlled within socially acceptable limits. This also applies negatively. In some residential situations individuals are excluded from contact with others far more than would be their choice. The common factor is that even when either takes place the number of people with whom the resident may make contact is strictly limited. Even where the residential unit is small and run on family lines, the selective choice is still minimal and without the natural bonds of affection that may make such restriction tolerable in a natural family.

Violence often takes the form of disruptive behaviour. The word 'disruptive' has negative connotations and should invite the question, 'Disruptive for whom?' Like deviance (p. 94), disruption is a judgement made by observers and relates specifically to their perception of the situation.

Sabath (1964) investigating the responses of groups to members who were seen as having high status in the group, found as follows:

(1) Individuals perceived as having high status were regarded more favourably than others. So behaviour that the group regarded as disruptive produced by these high-status individuals was not subjected to anything like the same level of adverse comment as similar behaviour produced by other members who did not have the same level of standing.

(2) Disruptive behaviour tends to be seen in the context of the behaviour preceding and following the disruptive episode. Thus when an individual creates disruption for the group, if this is followed by behaviour that produces benefit for the group, the individual concerned is liable to be regarded as a stimulating person. The group is also seen to gain an increase in satisfaction with their membership and to regard the stimulating/disruptive individual with favour. However, disruption followed by hindering behaviour produces the opposite effect, though a diverse one, of disfavour with the individual and dissatisfaction with membership.

(3) Even where disruption is negative, high-status members get away with it as far as the group is concerned because of a strong

tendency to discount the misbehaviour of high-status members. If this appears somewhat mystifying it must be remembered that high status is usually accorded to a group member largely because the group see him or her as being of greater than average value to the group in some way or other. Much can be forgiven members who can deliver the required goods in the time of group need.

This factor of the 'embedded' nature of violent acts has been noted by writers and practitioners in many forms of group-work. For example, Ainsworth and Fulcher say there is:

'no such thing as an aggressive child. . . . a complex interplay of personality facts and group dynamics located in a particular space/time context that combine to produce a specific behavioural result . . . the so-called "surface behaviour".'

(1981: 97)

Sherif (1976) suggested that the sufficient cause of much violent behaviour is the conflict generated by individuals and groups having goals that can be achieved only at the expense of other people. Raven and Rubin (1976) maintain that much violent behaviour results from frustration (the frustration/aggression/displacement thesis propounded by Dollard *et al.* 1939). The displacement factor is not just in terms of situation and person but in time also, so that suppressed responses to an anger-creating situation may be triggered by an entirely different situation often some distance in time from the original. This appears then to have come 'out of the blue', i.e. without any current precipitating factor, and is liable to be seen as coming from a violent personality.[2]

Raven and Rubin (1976) suggest that violent and aggressive behaviour divides into two categories: (1) hostile, where the primary purpose is to hurt, and (2) instrumental, where hurt occurs as a by-product of attempting to achieve some goal (see Sherif 1976, above). Jacobs and Spradlin (1974) remind us that aggression elicits aggression; Lazarus (1974) suggests that aggressive feelings are a major source of energy and can be used productively.

All the work on aggression and violence tends to highlight certain points:

(1) It may be deliberate because this has been found to be successful in the past in achieving goals.

(2) It may be related to learned behaviour in that it is an accepted response to the perception of certain kinds of situation.

(3) It may be related to the response to different people, situations, and times and bear small relationship to the circumstances in which it is expressed.

(4) The expression of violence tends to provoke an equally violent response.

Millham *et al.* (1981), in summing up their research into violence in residential settings, made the point that violence was seldom wanton, motiveless, or spasmodic. It is in essence a logical response to a situation as perceived by the violent person and is often a most appropriate one from their point of view. A considerable number of residents, i.e. people in residential situations, see themselves as probable victims of social violence through losing their liberty, having their privacy violated, being deprived of their social support systems, all of which they may not understand. In the world of the resident, the good intentions of others, usually more powerful, don't always make good sense, because different values prevail in which their possessors have invested just as much as we have in ours.

The whole question of violence throws up some major problems in the training of groupworkers and practitioners in residential settings, as we shall see later, but which are largely concerned with understanding our own responses when presented with disruptive or violent behaviour.

I would like to end this section with an illustration of a method of dealing with disruptive behaviour in a mental-hospital ward. The following description is a condensed version of work by Zinberg and Glotfelty (1968): A social groupworker was placed full-time on a mental-hospital ward in order to influence natural group formation and to utilize group values, norms, and forces in helping members move towards responsible adult concerns and ego integration. After six weeks' observation of twenty-one female patients, he was able to identify group formations, members, and group leaders. The socially disruptive patients were observed to be influencing other patients in a negative way by perpetuating self-destructive behaviour and discouraging relationships with staff. The groupworker made an informal relationship with the 'natural' leader of the patient group and working through her set up a programme of regular meetings to discuss the problems the group were facing and to attempt to find some solutions.

Zinberg and Glotfelty note that the process of influencing natural group formations was effective in reaching anti-social and anti-treatment behaviour patterns and in preventing their worsening and becoming permanent. In essence the disruptive behaviour was seen as stemming from a real perception on the part of the patients and was dealt with not at its face value of destructive behaviour, but at its roots by creating space and time for those root causes to be expressed.

It is interesting to note the length of time it took for the group worker to be sure that he had isolated the patterns of behaviour in a group of twenty-one patients in view of the speed with which most institutions believe such a review can be accomplished.

APATHY

Many statements have been made about apathy and in particular that the surface appearance of apathy can be produced by a wide variety of different underlying causes. Some quarter of a century ago Bradford, Stock, and Horwitz (1961) wrote a paper called 'How to Diagnose Group Problems', which I quoted in full in *Groupwork Practice* (Douglas 1976); this concerned the three most common group problems, i.e. conflict, apathy, and inadequate decision-making. As far as I am aware there has never been a better analysis of member apathy, and I make no excuses for drawing on it very heavily in this section.

Firstly, Bradford, Stock, and Horwitz list the ways in which apathy may be expressed, namely: frequent yawning, dozing off, members losing the point of what is being talked about, low level of participation, conversation drags, members come late to the group and are frequently absent, they are posturely flaccid and restless, decisions are made hastily with a marked absence of any action being taken on them, any excuse to quit the group session is valid, no effort is made to consider arrangements for the future, there is a marked reluctance to assume further responsibility.

The authors go on to give common reasons for group apathy:

(1) The focus of the group concern does not seem important to members or at least not as important as other concerns they may have.
(2) There may be good reasons why the group has no wish to achieve its 'stated' aims (e.g. it may mean moving on to the unfamiliar).
(3) The procedures available for dealing with the group task may be inadequate.
(4) Group members may feel they are powerless to influence final decisions.
(5) Conflict between some members has dominated group business to the extent that the rest no longer have any interest in the real task because they see no way of getting on with it.

Sometimes groups feel that they have a task that they can never achieve; it may lack clarity or it may be one that they find disturbing. Again, achieving some position in the group may be more important to members than what they are supposed to be trying to achieve. Some groups devote so much energy to maintaining themselves in existence that they have little or none to give to the task for which the group was originally created. Conflicts of loyalty may occur both within the group and with outside interests, and even conflict that is familiar may be more acceptable than achieving a goal that precipitates members into a new, unfamiliar, and therefore probably threatening situation.

Of course there are other reasons for apathy other than those relating to the situations in which group members find themselves and to which apathy is a response. For instance, members may be ill, tired, lacking in energy, bored, resentful, depressed, mentally or physically uncomfortable, and so on. As I have said many times, a wide variety of causes have a nasty habit of generating observable behaviour that is very similar. Apathy can be a conscious response, a kind of resistance, or a demonstration of an ability to control one's responses.

In Chapter 5 we will be looking at the group as a system that accepts and transforms energy. At the risk of pre-empting some of that material here it may be useful to consider apathy as a refusal to commit energy to the system or as a withdrawal of energy from it. In either case apathy results in a diminution of energy input into the group. Although in the case of a group other sources of energy may be available to it; the main result of diminishing energy is to reduce the satisfaction the members can gain from being part of the system. After some desperate efforts by highly committed (for whatever reason) members, the dullness and the reduction of satisfactions can spread by contagion, and the group disintegrates. If it has to continue in existence because its life span has been decreed by an authority over which the group can exercise no control, then either the group will be converted into something that generates satisfaction for the members in a different area to the legitimate one, or withdrawal of an all-embracing nature will occur.

Apathetic group members have to be encouraged to verbalize the causes of their lack of interest and not just in blanket phrases of being bored. Boredom is a manifestation and an expression of other factors, often of an inability to take what exists within a situation and use it to generate interest and satisfaction, probably arising from expectations that situations not immediately present as interesting within a limited context are intrinsically boring.

'The worst sin towards our fellow creatures is not to hate them, but to be indifferent to them, that's the essence of inhumanity.'
(G. B. Shaw, *The Devil's Disciple*, 1897)

SAFETY

Safety or a sense of security when in existence eliminates the anxiety of the perception of threat. When a person enters a group he or she is faced with what Goldbart and Cooper (1976) describe as a 'struggle' (see p. 187):

> 'upon entering group life, the individual is faced with two existential tasks: first, preserving his identity as an individual, and the manner in which he relates to others from his individual, autonomous perspective; second, the person's new role as a group member, the way he will define his group role, and relate to others from a group perspective.'
>
> (Goldbart and Cooper 1976: 240)

There is often conflict between personal safety, which dictates caution, and the need to be accepted so that the benefits of being a group member can be enjoyed, which dictates the production of the right form of acceptable behaviour. People coming into groups are already either secure people for whom new situations present interest but not threat, or insecure people who have developed techniques for coping with their insecure state and who may be alarmed by the possibilities existing within the unknown situation of the exposure of the inadequacies of those techniques.

In a thesis that is a statement of a kind of group safety sequence, Goldbart and Cooper (1976) present four ways in which a group may develop safety. The sequence goes as follows:

(1) The struggle to establish safety both for members as individuals and in order to generate a group identity that absorbs the energy and activity of a group in its initial stages.

(2) As the potential dangers become more explicit then the group tends to develop activities and behaviours that protect the individual member's identity. The maintenance factor is very important, and the group becomes absorbed with structures – safety resides in knowing where you are as defined by some clearly understood and commonly shared rules, norms, and values.

(3) The group begins to develop a knowledge and understanding of group processes, not directly from its own behaviour

but from information sources outside the group, even though these may be conveyed to the group by its own members. Safety resides in the distance between the knowing-about-groups and one's actual existence within one.

(4) By developing strategies of avoidance a group may generate a sense of safety.

All these methods are relevant to different stages of a group's development and ultimately should lead to a safety that is dependent wholly upon the ability of members to predict the kinds of response they will elicit. As experience of each other grows, sufficient evidence should accumulate of the kinds of risk that can be taken with impunity and those that it may be possible to take later. The methods of dealing with inappropriate responses, of dealing with hurt, and of pushing back the boundaries of what is acceptable and accepted, will have been noted and either openly or tacitly agreed on. In short, what groupwork texts are fond of calling 'trust' will have developed.

All the other methods should lead to this at an appropriate level for the life of the group. If they do not, but become fixed, then they will inhibit the growth of the group and reduce the level of satisfaction of members. 'Processes which were initiated by people to ensure safety threaten to become the very traps which make work in a group impossible' (Goldbart and Cooper 1976: 255).

DECISION-MAKING

All groups have to make decisions. It is relatively easy to ignore the fact that one major decision which can be made is not to make any decisions. In essence this means not making any overt decisions but responding directly to what happens; thus a very major decision has been taken.

Decision-making in groups has always fascinated writers and researchers — because the process by which groups come to conclusions is seldom clearly understood by the members of the group. Indeed many group members are subsequently at a loss as to how they appear to have agreed to decisions without actually being aware that they had done so. Sometimes the circumstances in which the decisions are sought may enhance this process – as when, for example, at a recent meeting of dock workers the workers came away from the meeting after a show of hands convinced that they had voted overwhelmingly to go to work, only to find that the union officials had declared the meeting to be in favour of a strike. Anticipation of the result in this case and the pressure to conform might well have led to a miscount of the displayed hands.

However, the general nature of the decision-making processes is well covered in previous texts (see, for instance, Collins and Guetzkow 1964, Raven and Rubin 1976). In this section I shall deal with factors that affect the quality of group decisions.

Steiner (1974) noted four major factors affecting the nature of group decisions:

(1) Accepting the most popular option.
(2) The status of members favouring a particular option.
(3) Compliance, based upon the perception by members of the ability of the option-proposers or -favourers to deliver rewards or punishments.
(4) Confidence, which affects the way views are presented, confident performance being deemed more likely to gain acceptance.

Janis (1972) had already concluded that bad group decisions could be prevented by the following:

(1) The information available within the group about the problem under consideration could be made explicit – which may need some careful handling so that possessors of information could feel able to communicate what they knew.
(2) The attractive nature of popular options and those favoured by high-status members should also be made explicit.
(3) The arrival at agreement could be postponed until all minority opinions had been expressed and given serious attention.

(4) The high-status members should not be allowed to intimidate those of lesser status within the group.
(5) The less confident members should be encouraged in the expression of their ideas.

There are some additional ideas about the factors affecting the quality of group decisions that are worthy of consideration. For instance, where a group accepts a common purpose, the possibility of co-ordinated effort is much more likely, and the exchange of relevant information is usually at a good level. The way decision-making may be pursued is directly related to the factors of time and task. Thus where the task is known and relatively simple and the time to complete it is unalterably short, decision-making must proceed under a restrictive structure so that none of the scarce resources are wasted in irrelevant procedures. Conversely with ample time and faced with a decision of some complexity a restrictive structure for the decision-making process would almost certainly produce an inefficient performance and a bad decision.

The effects related to group size can be discovered elsewhere (e.g. Hare 1962, chapter 8: 224–45; Douglas 1979: 87–9).

What Janis (1972) called 'group think' is a constellation of factors that inevitably lead to bad group decisions. They were as follows:

(1) The illusion of invulnerability and superior morality; a general sense among group members of being better, stronger, etc. than others.
(2) The illusion of unanimity; when the group members make statements like 'We must all agree', believing this in fact to be so with no real evidence.
(3) Personal doubts are suppressed, e.g. 'If I disagree with the others I must be wrong.'
(4) Pressures towards uniformity:

    (a) the fewer deviants the greater the pressure for uniformity;
    (b) the more relevant any opinion is to the participants the greater the pressure;

    (c) the more cohesive the group the greater the pressure;

    (d) the greater the presence among members of the group of personality factors such as authoritarian rigidity, low self-esteem, self-blaming, high need of acceptance, lower intelligence, anxiety, low tolerance of ambiguity, the greater the pressure.

(5) Self-appointed people who coerce others into line (Janis called these group members 'mind guards').

(6) Docility fostered by suave leadership.

In combination these factors produced 'a deterioration of mental efficiency, reality testing and moral judgement that results from in-group pressure' (Janis 1972: 9).

The factors affecting group decisions must be of concern to all in a group-living situation, but of the two major sub-groups within any residential establishment the staff must be the more concerned. The decisions they make affect not just themselves and their immediate colleagues, but the lives and the quality of existence of all those in their care. Added to the factors listed so far are the effects of tradition, of the norms of the group, of contagion, of the pressure of the majority, and of example. Any decision made in a staff group could be influenced by any of these, and because they tend to be decisions about others consideration of their possible effects is morally a necessity.

The usual formulation of decision-making processes could be improved, as Janis (1972) says, by the information available to the group being made explicit. However, exactly the opposite problem sometimes prevents a group from making good decisions:

'such a synoptic or comprehensive attempt at problem-solving is not possible to the degree that clarification of objectives founders on social conflict, that required information is either not available or available only at prohibitive cost, or that the problem is simply too complex for man's finite intellectual capacities. Its complexity may stem from an impossibly large number of alternative policies and their possible repercussions, from imponderables in the delineation of

objectives even in the absence of social disagreement on them, *from a supply of information too large to process in the mind*, or from still other causes.'
(Hirschman and Lindblom 1962: 211–22) (emphasis added)

Added to the dimension of not making a decision at all, this suggests that there is the need for attacking problems, of bringing the ends within the scope of the means available, of allowing for the incompleteness of information that will nearly always exist instead of seeking for some 'rational' completeness. This is no excuse for not bothering or for not using the methods that will disclose what material is available, but simply means recognizing the quality of whatever decision is arrived at.

Like most activities in which groups indulge, decision-making has to strike a balance in accord with the realities of the situation. Many times I have seen group members attempting to achieve aims including decisions that any observer could see were not possible with the resources available, at least not in the manner or at the level at which the attempt was being made. Decisions in residential situations are liable to affect many people's lives markedly. Decisions made by groups are noted for being riskier (see Walker 1974) than those made by individuals; they are safer for those who make them but perhaps they are more dangerous for those who are the subject of decisions.

One further point needs to be made about group decision-making concerning the personalities of the group members and the operating rules by which the group functions:

'When pressures for conformity and consensus are either explicitly or implicitly incorporated into the rules of the group, there is a strong likelihood that the decision will be determined by the person who possesses the most dominant personality. But where the group operates under a more pluralistic form of decision-making, with dissents freely permitted to the group decision, both medium dominant and high dominant personalities will be about equally influential, and low dominant personalities will perhaps play a larger role in the decision process.'

(Scioli, Dyson, and Fleitas 1974: 19)

Dominant personalities are often the designated leaders in groups, and if they should be running a group where the rules insist on agreement and on accepted behaviour, they are likely to make all the major decisions. Where there is freedom to question the rules, and agreement is not wholly expected, then there is much more certainty that most members will contribute to any decision-making process. It depends on what is required, what the group seeks to achieve, whether the situation under which the group operates will support achievement or not (see p. 51 concerning status).

TERRITORIALITY

Animal studies over a number of years have shown the importance of territoriality – that is, the ability to define a given area of space as one's own and to defend it against intrusion. The amount of such space that an animal requires and can successfully maintain is related both to its needs and to its status and power within the social group. As a result of studies of territoriality a direct relationship between it and aggression was sought and also any indications that human beings might be involved in some form of territorial behaviour (Altman 1970).

In studying the effect of crowding upon behaviour, Freedman (1975) showed that human beings, unlike animals, have methods of compensating for lack of personal space and that density of population may not therefore be such a direct cause of aggressive and violent behaviour as might have been thought. Yet again some researchers, e.g. Kinze (1971), have sought to show that there is a direct link between possessing a large personal space (that area surrounding one's physical body, which in some way we seem to regard as ours and invasion of which without invitation causes anxiety and often anger) and violent behaviour.

DeLong (1973) showed that territoriality occurred at specific times during the life of a group and was not necessarily a consistent phenomenon. His research indicated that territoriality was related to the need for stability, and thus it became a much more dominant feature of group life when aggression within the group was reaching high levels of intensity. DeLong went on to adduce that staking out a territorial claim and maintaining it during periods of disturbance was an assertion of a leadership capability. In group dynamic theory the appearance of stability has usually been associated with members of the higher levels of dominance in any group.

Before pursuing these facts further it is necessary to note that territoriality in a group-living situation may be individual or group centred. Edney and Uhlig (1977) see the purpose of each as being very different. For instance, individual territorial claims are concerned to isolate the claimant from others; group territorial claims assert the uniting factor of possession. The individual asserts that total possession is his or hers; group territoriality indicates a desire to share. Also, individual territoriality not only asserts independence but emphasizes personal distinctiveness, whereas group territoriality indicates dependence and anonymity. The authors say that the difference between individual and group territoriality is like the difference between individual identity and groupness:

> 'a person's act of dissolving his individual territory boundaries, so as to bond with other individuals, may mean a forfeiture of identity for the sake of strength and group unity.'
> (Edney and Uhlig 1977: 458)

This study found that while territorial possession has advantages it also has certain costs in terms of the worry and responsibility of holding territory. What emerged clearly was that individuals felt a stronger sense of ownership of the environment when alone than as part of a group. This sense that others are responsible finds a large echo in the material on bystander apathy,[3] which shows that people in groups tend to abdicate responsibility for action in a crisis because they feel that there are others who will accept it. Individuals tend to respond much more readily to a crisis; there is no one else immediately at hand on whom to load responsibility.

Other findings from Edney and Uhlig's (1977) research may be listed as follows:

(1) The behaviour of people was attributed by them more to the influence of their environment, especially to their home

ground, than others would. (This also links in very closely with the research findings of Jones and Nisbett (1971), that actors in a situation ascribe most of their behaviour to being a response to that situation as they see it, while observers see the actors' behaviour as stemming from personality factors.)

(2) Territoriality is a means of establishing freedom by controlling the admission of others.

(3) Group territoriality may be the basis of group identity – the common factor of the possession of territory.

One further factor needs to be presented. Throughout this discussion territoriality has been presented as being a matter of ownership of part of the environment. But we must also consider that territorial claims can exist in certain kinds of behaviour, in given topics, or in selected services. It is possible, for instance, for leadership to be seen as a territorial right.

The deliberate or unwitting infringement of territorial rights is one of the surest ways to provoke an aggressive response. Because territoriality is directly related to an individual's or a group's independence and self-esteem, such an incursion poses a great threat in much the same way that invasion of personal space provokes either withdrawal or confrontation.

In group living the whole factor of crowding becomes important, though as Freedman (1975) noted sheer density of occupancy does not of itself necessarily lead to the proliferation of stress. Other factors, such as heat, smells, the amount of air available, cleanliness, how much need there is to move around, whether the individual is present voluntarily or not, the length of time spent in these conditions, the sense of injustice, imposition, or unfairness especially in comparison with others, and the physical and mental health of the individual, all contribute to the outcome.

On pp. 100–05 we shall look more closely at the way dominance and territoriality have been found to influence the behaviour of boys in a residential institution.

INDIVIDUAL- AND GROUP-CONTROLLING BEHAVIOUR

Group analysts have always been fascinated by the ways in which individual members of a group use manipulative skills to control group outcomes in their favour. Goffman (1968, 1969a, 1969b), Berne (1964), and Shostrom (1967) have all been concerned with the manipulation of symbols, the games that are played. Eventually Christie and Geis (1970) developed a method of measuring the different degrees of what they called Machiavellianism, defined as the 'willingness to manipulate others'.

> 'In addition to possessing the interpersonal style of the manipulator, High Machs[4] are excessively task-oriented and treat others as objects to be controlled rather than individuals with whom they can develop harmonious relationships.'
>
> (Bochner, Di Salvo, and Jonas 1975: 188)

Conversely there are group members, low on the Machiavellian characteristics, who are emotional, get involved in irrelevant interaction, and respond affectively to situations.

What emerges as interesting is how these people with high manipulative intent exert their influence upon the group process. One clear way would seem to be their use of communication, particularly of verbal communications. Bochner, Di Salvo, and Jones (1975) put forward three facts from their research as follows:

(1) The high manipulator is always amongst the most frequent participators in the group.
(2) He or she is the most important contributor of information related specifically to whatever task the group is performing. Therefore he or she has the most significant influence on the formation of the data base that the group uses in the accomplishment of its task.
(3) There may be some correlation between the frequency with which he or she uses words that are significant and the group's decision-making process.

In summary, high-level manipulators would seem to influence and control the behaviour of groups of which they are members by flooding the group with extremely relevant and useful information during critical periods of the processes of discussion and decision-making. Some secondary points are that these group members also tended to be sensitive to their surroundings, the timing of their interventions is good, and they appear to be aware when the group needs structure.

Without doubt this piece of research has substantiated what many groupworkers and researchers had already discovered about the skills some group members have to manipulate their peers into producing those results that are favourable to the manipulator. Verbal communication is not the only method, but the researchers have clearly spelled out for us the ways in which it has been done.

I think there are two crucial pieces of learning to be obtained from this research for those working in a group-living situation:

(1) Close observation of the nature, quality, and frequency of comment by individual group members, particularly at critical information-needing times, should serve to indicate which individuals are seeking to influence the outcome most strongly and effectively. If the direction this influence is taking is a beneficial one, then it can be either encouraged or left alone; if it is seen as being harmful, it can be modified or stopped; and, since in each case the source of influence has been identified, the appropriate measures can be applied to that source by exposing it.

(2) Verbal communication skilfully directed at information-giving during crucial periods of group decision-making can be an acquired leadership technique as well as the normal function of the task-oriented manipulative personality. As a deliberate intervention employed to influence the direction and decision-making of a group, it needs to be used with the same degree of situational sensitivity that seems to be the stock-in-trade of the 'natural' manipulator.

In 1953 William H. Haythorn attempted to chart the relationship between the individual member's behaviour and the characteristics of the total group. He was looking to see what influence individual behaviour had on the group. He decided his results were 'highly tentative', but they are interesting enough to be worth studying here. He found that:

'Individuals who are chosen by co-workers as good leaders or as persons with whom others like to work, "facilitate" group functioning, while individuals who "depress" group functioning are not generally chosen by other members of the group.'

'Individual behavior patterns which include co-operativeness, efficiency and insight . . . tend to "facilitate" or be positively related to effective group functioning.'

'Individual behavior patterns which include aggressiveness, self-confidence, initiative, interest in individual solution, and authoritarianism . . . tend to be somewhat negatively related to ratings of group cohesiveness and friendliness' (see p. 147).

'Sociable behavior . . . tends to reduce group motivation and competition, but to increase group talkativeness, friendliness [see p. 147] and interest in social action.'

'Personality traits involving maturity, adaptability, and acceptance of others [see p. 140] tend to be positively related to smooth and effective group functioning.'

'Personality traits involving suspiciousness, eccentricity and coolness towards others tend to be negatively related to smooth group functioning.'

(Haythorn 1953: 283–84)

There are some very interesting correlations here, not least that self-confident behaviour on the part of a group member is inhibiting of friendliness within the group and has a similar constraining effect upon the development of group bond. But the main point of Haythorn's discussion was not these correlations in themselves but what this might mean in terms of leadership. After all, leader behaviour is only the most obvious form of group-limiting exercised by the individual.

If group functioning is related to the production of certain kinds of individual behaviour, then control of specific forms of individual behaviour can be used as an indirect means of influencing group function. There is nothing new in this. For example, behaviour that is labelled as 'disturbing' or 'inhibiting' has always been subjected to some control attempt by those who see it as part of their function to ensure, as far as possible, that the group achieves its aims. The difference with Hay-thorn's correlations is that they are not obvious and thus not understood and or used. In some ways they equal the prescriptive nature of Feldman's work (1967 and 1969), where the author tries to show that intervention can be based upon research materials; for example:

'If . . . a group worker wished to increase a given member's integration into the group (that is, to increase the individual's liking for the group's members and to increase their liking for him), an effective focus for worker intervention would appear to be the member's capacity to perform necessary functions for the group.'

(Feldman 1967: 51)

It may be common sense to say that demonstrable usefulness generates acceptance and that the implications are far-reaching. For instance, the worker must know that the member's re-sources, skills, knowledge, and ability are available; he or she must also know what the needs of the group are. This kind of knowledge is not lying around for anyone to pick up at random; it has to be worked for and used as part of the facilitative process with a particular group. Resources that exist within the gestalt of group and leader(s) can be used only if:

(1) their presence is known;
(2) a situation can be created in which they can be made available with minimum anxiety; and
(3) the needs of the group, which require the use of these resources, are not only known but also explicit to all.

Tapping resources, as we shall see, is a highly skilled but extremely rewarding piece of leader behaviour, whoever carries it out.

DEVIANCE

Schur (1979) suggested that all that was really essential for deviance to exist was that some behaviour or some people should provoke negative reactions in others, who would then express their response and may even take some action. Thus Schur's proposition is that there are no such persons as deviants but there are those whose behaviour is regarded as deviant by others when compared to the generally accepted norms. While we are not concerned here with general deviant behaviour, Schur's definition is wholly applicable to the kinds of behaviour that are referred to as 'deviant' in small groups. Furthermore, as in all matters relating to group behaviour, there is the ubiquitous interrelatedness of major factors. Thus 'deviant' behaviour is related to sanctions, and the latter to the status of the deviants.

Wahrman pointed out that much of the previous research on deviant behaviour and the response to it had in fact omitted to concern itself with the nature and seriousness of the deviant acts: 'they focussed on behaviour threatening the identity or integrity of the group or significantly jeopardizing important group goals' (Wahrman 1977: 164). He postulated that the response to deviant behaviour depended to some extent upon the degree to which it was seen by the other members as seriously threatening the survival of the group.

Previous research had also ignored the effect that discussion in the group of the 'deviant' behaviour might have on the outcome. As Wahrman says, this resulted from the experimental nature of the groups involved, and he shows that in non-experimental groups discussion does take place. When non-conforming behaviour occurs, group members try to understand it, and attempt to assess its meaning by consulting one another and noting individual responses. The end point is reached when the group as a unit decides on an effective interpretation of the behaviour and on a response to it. Neither of these outcomes is essentially predictable from the response of individuals.

This unit response can occur only in a group which has developed the capability to work together that is a product not just of the time spent together but also of the degree to which energy has been diverted from individuals' need to protect themselves to pursuing some part of the group's goals. In simple terms a level of trust has developed that is compatible with working together. Even in this state high-status members and the most vociferous will have a considerable effect on the outcomes.

Another factor affecting the outcome of the discussion of deviant behaviour, universally recognized but not well understood, is the effect of 'polarization'. To quote Warhman again:

> 'Rather consistently it has been found that group discussion makes individual judgements more extreme in the direction toward which they were initially moving — i.e. cautious judgements become more cautious, risky judgements become more risky, groups of relatively unprejudiced people become less prejudiced, groups of prejudiced people become more prejudiced and so on.'
>
> (Warhman 1977: 150)

Brown (1965) suggested that this effect occurs because group members need to appear at least as committed to the group as others. The ultimate result is that where groups follow their usual method of discussing 'deviant' behaviour, there is an intensification of pre-existing attitudes, a shift.

Warhman discovered, however, that discussion about deviant behaviour produced harsher evaluations of that behaviour than would have been the case without discussion but reduced the severity of the sanctions, which implies that other factors must be involved. What immediately offers is that loyalty to peers supersedes the upholding of group norms. Thus the evaluation is tough, but the sanctions that might decrease a member's satisfaction with his or her membership too drastically are not applied, and the severity is usually positively correlated with the degree of threat to group security. High-status members are neither more leniently nor more harshly treated than others when the 'serious' rating of their behaviour is not high.

So both the production of 'deviant' behaviour and the response to it within the group can be truly understood only if seen as embedded in, and arising from, the group itself. Change, new thinking, new action, and new direction may all originate as 'deviant' behaviour, i.e. disturbing the established harmony of the group's procedures. Given that the group has progressed beyond the point where responses could be expected to retain large elements of personal and individual safety, then the methods of handling deviant behaviour have to take account of the potential value of the 'deviants'. What is more, those methods must also contain two messages for future deviants: firstly, that such behaviour will be evaluated and punished; but also, secondly, that the punishment will be related to perceived value and thus will not be such as will deter anyone from deviant behaviour that will probably have a positive outcome.

This delicate decision is often quite clearly made. Thus a group member with considerable value for the group will be permitted to behave in outrageous ways provided that his or her behaviour does not threaten group security. Anger will be displayed, and clashes will occur, but they will stop well below the line of serious punishment. To outside observers such behaviour often appears to indicate an intolerable level of presumption on the part of the deviant and a very timid acceptance on the part of the group. Such is the difference between detached observation and the perception of the deeply involved.

CONFORMITY

'Trumpet in a herd of elephants, crow in the company of cocks, bleat in a flock of goats.'

(Malay proverb)

In essence conformity implies behaviour that falls within the accepted norms of any group, large or small.[5]

Some conformity is essential for any group to function, but too much conformity generates stagnation and the absence of new ideas and thus of change. As will be stated many times throughout this text, conformity can also be genuine in the sense that the norms are wholly internalized by the individual, or it can be spurious, an effort to survive in a relatively and perhaps truly hostile environment from which there is no apparent avenue of escape.

Groups are notorious for exerting conformity pressures: for example, the boy who has been as well behaved as could be expected, who then becomes an accepted member of a gang and whose behaviour changes ('deteriorates', his parents would perhaps say) in accord with the standard patterns of his new-found peer group. This illustration contains all the classic ingredients. Patterns of conformity are instilled as part of the process of growing up. They tend originally to be set by the family and thus are acceptable to that group. But as experience of other groups grows their different norms are encountered, and so the overall pattern of conformity behaviour changes and adapts. Adoption of the norms of other groups is usually effected only when the individual believes that the group can meet some of his or her current needs. People pay the price of acceptance to get what they believe they want by behaving in accordance with group norms. Should their needs change, or should an opportunity for the same, nearly the same, or even greater satisfaction offer elsewhere for less cost, they will move. This statement needs only to be considered in the light of the probable behaviour of those placed in groups not of their own choosing, whose norms are not to their liking, where the costs of remaining are remarkably high and from which no escape is permitted, to realize how important it may be in the analysis of residential behaviour.

From the foregoing it would seem that the need to be accepted by a group or a perception that being accepted will bring high levels of reward produces behaviour that is acceptable to the group, i.e. conforming behaviour. But as could be expected other factors have some influence on levels of conformity. Feldman (1974) found in children that smaller groups had higher proportions of conformers than larger groups, probably related to the visibility of behaviour in small groups; and that environmental factors influence the degree of conformity, probably by establishing an ethos in which there is a high level of expectation of conformity. Bonney (1974) suggested that conformity was related to the degree of cohesiveness in a group, which in essence implies that conformity is a product of satisfaction with the group.

As we shall note several times in this book, a distinction has to be drawn between two different kinds of conformity both of which produce behaviour that is superficially identical. But in the management of people the base upon which conformity rests is of crucial importance, so any clues that might define the differences are crucial.

Often enough the distinction that is made is between public and private conformity or acceptance. In public, group members will conform to the group's standards of behaviour because they know they will be punished for not doing so. If there are alternative groups to which they can escape, then their level of conformity will be low; if there are no alternatives of escape, then the level of conformity will depend upon the individual's assessment of the costs and rewards existing in the situation for him or her. In essence public conformity is a security exercise for the individual grounded in the fear of sanctions.

The other form of conformity results from a whole-hearted acceptance by the individual of the major part of the group's norms. No sanctions are necessary to keep this behavioural pattern in place; the individual would like to behave in this way, group or no group. What delights him or her is to find support for his or her behaviour from like-minded peers. It is possible to transfer from public to private acceptance/conformity; in fact this is precisely what all attempts to change people are really about. Essentially change is brought about by exposure to different methods of behaving in a supportive and non-threatening atmosphere in the hope that increased levels of reward from the new behaviours will bring about their freely accepted adoption.

Those factors that seem to identify private acceptance as distinct from public conformity relate to the satisfaction a member receives from his or her membership of the group. Thus members with high levels of commitment to the group — those who find the group attractive, its rules acceptable, its goals agreeable, its confidence high, and their own status equally so — are not likely to conform out of fear of sanctions. The more individuals' behaviour coincides with the expectations of the group in giving them pleasure, the greater will be their private acceptance of the group as a unit that confirms them, their ideas, beliefs, and practices.

Those factors that identify public conformity appear wholly dissociated from pleasure and reward and seem to relate entirely to the tensions brought about by having to sustain unavoidable and unacceptable costs. There is a clear realization that without the sanctions against non-conforming behaviour the individual's behaviour would be markedly different, and there should be evidence that he or she finds the restraints irksome. Many public conformers are to be found on the periphery of groups as far out as they dare go without bringing down the wrath of the group on their heads. They keep the rules just as much as is necessary to survive and they are as a consequence seldom trusted or given anything but the lowest tasks and status. This cyclic effect is very hard to break through even for those on the outskirts of a group who have a change of heart and want to move in.

BEHAVIOUR IN RESIDENTIAL GROUPS

It is no accident that the behaviour pattern presented first in this chapter was the one that shows as violent or disruptive. As I said in that section, many people who find themselves in a residential situation must have a strong sense that social violence of some sort has been committed on them; if understanding is lacking, there is obvious reason for violent behaviour in speech or action against those most readily accessible to be hurt.

Just as groups can inspire and create violence, they can support their members through violence, and they can also generate a supportive system that will allow the expression of violence with minimal hurt and disseminate understanding about its causes. A good balanced attempt to understand violence in residential settings is to be found in Millham *et al.*'s (1981) study of community homes. It is interesting to note when discussing group violence how many of the listed precipitating factors are related to the major group processes. Violence is more likely when:

(1)　new disruptive elements are admitted (see p. 187);
(2)　old stabilizing ones are discharged

(3) the formation of cliques of difficult residents with griev-
ances occurs (see p. 60);
(4) a poor communication system exists between staff and
residents (see p. 59);
(5) there is a change from a strict to a more permissive regime;
(6) there is staff disunity;
(7) there are increases in staff anxiety;
(8) there are inadequate numbers of staff, or rapid changes are
occurring;
(9) contagion develops into a self-perpetuating system.

This all adds up to the fact that violent behaviour is a response,
and a logical one from the point of view of the actor, to the situation. As we have seen (p. 88), the observer's response to such
behaviour is very likely to be provoked by his or her perception
that it stems from the personality traits of the actor — discrepancy in the perception of causation that does not improve the
possibility of understanding.

Apathy tends to be a response based upon perceptions that
the situation cannot be changed, that it is not worth the effort to
try, or that the whole scene has no interest or value as far as the
individual is concerned. The investment of energy therefore is
dramatically reduced on the wholly logical basis of an estimate
of value. Of course apathy sometimes stems from illness or
exhaustion, but in these cases the evidence of causation is
usually reasonably clear. When apparent apathy is also accompanied by gross hostility, then the situation is very different.
This is no lack of energy; this is an active, aggressive withdrawal
of commitment or a refusal to give it as a protest. There is not
the essential spirit of hopelessness that characterizes genuine
apathy.

The fundamental points to make about apathy in a residential
group are:

(1) It is a clear indication of how the situation looks to the
individual and is not to be confused with an expression of
hostile opposition.
(2) In the confines of a residential setting it can become a focus
for other kinds of dissent and opposition.

(3) Likewise the closeness of contact in such a setting ensures that some element of contagion is possible.

(4) Apathetic members in an otherwise active group display such a level of difference that they are liable to be scapegoated by other members, particularly if their apathy is seen as holding the group back from some form of progress or achievement.

It may be that the basic cause of apathy, i.e. residence in the particular setting, cannot be changed, in which case it is essential that attempts to induce energy output in some acceptable (if any) area of the situation should be encouraged. But it is equally important that such efforts should be carefully monitored for the level of frustration that might arise, which could lead directly to the implementation of the behaviour pattern in (4) above.

The factor of safety occurs in many forms throughout this book and is often described as being related to the ability to predict responses. But it is also related to familiarity. We tend to forget that strangeness can be tolerated in normal existence in so far as it does not assume too large a proportion of our experience. The familiar, the anchors, the landmarks that are a large part of the way we make sense of our lives are 'stabilizers' and form a balance heavily weighted in favour of 'usefulness'. Thus the proportion of change is a crucial factor in our adjustment. Many people who become part of a residential establishment tend to exchange familiarity for almost total unfamiliarity; hence they attempt as quickly as possible to establish contact with those elements of the new situation that have some resemblance to what was familiar previously. This is often discovered in the experience of others, familiar objects, routines, habits, etc. But the essential familiarity for all of us resides inside ourselves, and it is no accident that when the outside world becomes unfamiliar, and the attempt to adjust to it yet again seems to pose an exorbitant cost in terms of energy for apparently minimal reward, individuals withdraw into themselves, into what may seem to be the sole remaining haven of familiarity.

This kind of withdrawal is common enough amongst old people but it can equally be found amongst all ages. Given the amount of energy available in the younger age groups, however, and the lack of repetitive experience of trying to integrate, the sheer proportion of unfamiliarity has to be of a high order usually in order to precipitate such a response.

One of the more important and perhaps least understood functions of a group concerns the decisions it takes. An almost universal experience of working with groups is the limited knowledge members have of how a particular decision of their group came to be made. Thus the whole process of decision-making covering every aspect of group life has to be consciously analysed to reveal the principles and methods involved. Factors such as the willingness with which the group members uphold and maintain decisions in which they have been involved, and the sense of grievance, resentment, and discontent or anger that may result from being compelled to abide by decisions imposed, are both part of the reason for a necessary understanding of the decision-making process. One definition of powerlessness has always been that state in which decisions are taken affecting crucial aspects of an individual's life over which he or she has not the slightest influence.

Control is directly related to the ability and authority to make decisions. Huge collections of people can be directed by individuals and by small groups, provided units of that collection do not sink their individuality and combine to form a decision-making body in their own right. This situation is often prevented by the simple process of maintaining separateness between individuals, usually by some kind of conflict or competitiveness.

The confined space of any residential community can serve to highlight the problems of territoriality. As we have seen, it is relatively easy for an individual in an unfamiliar setting to make his or her first bid for safety in claiming some form of territorial right, e.g. his chair, her position, or a piece of floor-space. Apparent trivia can become invested with fantastic importance in this way. Concomitant with territoriality is the concept of privacy. This is especially so when culturally privacy has been an important fact and where habit has engendered an essential privacy as the basis of safety. Evidence in plenty shows that human beings have become accustomed to, and are often supported by, high-density living situations. But then an element of choice has been available, if not in whether one lives in a high-density area then regarding with whom one associates within it. Residential situations frequently eliminate or at least reduce both these choices, and so choice and safety have to be attached to something else.

Control factors in terms of manipulative behaviour require others to be available to be manipulated, and residential situations provide plenty of material. There are many people who have learnt that survival in a social situation can come about seemingly only if they exercise skill in the manipulation of others. In a residential setting the staff sub-group may well exercise power in this way. Groupworkers are often designated as manipulators, and some clients, because of the learning provided by their experience, also become manipulative. The point under consideration is not really the manipulation itself – after all, it is a common experience of everyday life – but the intent and the conscious awareness of intent with which it is done are what matters. All 'natural' leaders emerge because they are able to demonstrate some kind of manipulative behaviour that appears to be of value to their peers.

What tends to arise from this kind of behaviour within the confines of a residential setting is a conflict between various manipulating individuals. Dominating behaviour is then seen by designated leaders not so much as a response to a situation but as a straight personality trait or confrontation, and motives of hostility are accorded to it that may be completely at odds with what the behaviour really deserves.

The last two group behaviour patterns are often seen as opposite sides of the same coin. Conformity, whatever its basic motivation, certainly ensures a smoothly flowing organization; deviance does not. But a major problem in large organizations resides in the choice of conforming to this or that pattern of behaviour. Conformity levels are often very high to the immediate small group and minimal to the standards of the larger containing organization. The reasons for this are not hard to find. In large organizations the discovery of deviance is significantly less probable in the organization as a whole unless very marked, but it is absolutely certain in the smaller sub-group. Following from this is the fact that punishment from the small group is liable to be immediate, very effective, and relatively harsh, because one deviant member represents a significant loss to the group in terms of morale, energy, and effectiveness. Punishment from the large organization is seldom immediate, often ineffective, and usually lenient unless the element of threat to the organization is of a much higher order than usual. Thus conformity to the immediate group is perhaps a greater demand on the individual than conformity to the larger organization.

Although conformity and deviance are seen as important or not according to the proportion of their occurrence in relation to the size of the group, deviance often has positive factors as well as negative. Conformity behaviour seldom if ever produces challenge, new ideas, or impetus for change, and can thus bring about a kind of complacent stagnation. Deviant behaviour can sometimes reveal weak points, opening up different and, it is hoped, better ways of doing things. It is often resisted because change requires effort and is frequently threatening, because established (and therefore comfortable) patterns of behaviour have to be broken and others established.

Many of the points about the group behaviours mentioned in this chapter and their relevance to group living are reasonably explicit. What I have attempted to do is to make some beginning connections that can be pursued much further and given a specific direction by anyone with sufficient experience and interest.

NOTES

1 For a good presentation of this point and of the available research, see Aronson 1980, chapter 2.
2 There are many theories about aggression and violence. See Tutt 1976.
3 For a good discussion of bystander apathy, see Eysenck and Eysenck 1981, chapter 1.

4 With the social scientist's penchant for coining phraseology and then abbreviating it, High and Low Machs are people who have high or low scores on the Christie–Geis (1970) measurement of Machiavellianism.

5 An excellent account of most of the general ideas about conformity occurs in Aronson 1980, chapter 2: 13–49.

5 Leadership

'Our analysis . . . suggest[s] that in emphasising the effect of leadership, we may be overlooking far more powerful environmental influences. Unless leadership is studied as part of a total set of forces, one cannot gauge its impact. Moreover, the leadership effect may vary greatly between goals in an organisation.'

(Lieberson and O'Connor 1972: 298)

Lieberson and O'Connor set out to discover 'the relative importance of leadership and organisational environment for organisational outcome' (1972: 284). What they discovered in part echoes a basic theme of this book: that it is unwise to attempt in isolation understanding of any particular dynamic of either large complex organizations or small face-to-face groups. Leadership patterns in small groups may be much more clearly recognized as influencing the outcome of the group, not because small-group leaders are more effective than leaders of large complex organizations, but because the size and complexity of the latter absorb leader effort and exert a constraining influence that is infinitely more massive than can be mustered in a small group.

Take just the factor of time of communication. In a small group most communications are immediate. This needs some explanation, because it does tend to beg the question in that communication is usually accepted as having occurred only when a message has been sent in some form or other and the sender has received at least a response of acknowledgement from the receiver. Some people would argue that this acknowledgement should contain some indication that the message has been understood before they would assert that communication had taken place. Accepting this point, it is possible to say that the presentation of communication in a small group is made in the presence of those to whom it is addressed, which permits the immediate perception that it has been received and the immediate possibility of checking what level of understanding may have been gained.

In a large complex organization only a small part of the organization's overall communication system is of the nature of small-group communication; most of it has to be by methods of communication that diminish the immediacy of perception and of checking any response, or that reduce the intensity of contact between communicators, or both (see p. 59). This must inevitably open up the possibility of everything from assumed understanding, through distortion, to complete lack of understanding occurring. Given that any form of leadership must be largely based upon the ability to communicate effectively, then it would be only reasonable to expect that the larger organizations would have a diminishing effect on the effectiveness of leadership unless some stringent precautions to preserve accuracy of communication were taken.

There are of course other factors that reduce leadership influence in large complex organizations – for example, the formal structure, regulations, policy-makers and policy, the economic state of society, technological factors, the fashionableness or otherwise of the organization and its function, and so on; the list is endless. Lieberson and O'Connor noted that these environmental constraints did not have the same effects on leadership over all parts of a system. Some were much more affected by one or more of the constraints than others; some seemed to be almost free of any other than the innate or acquired leadership qualities of the leaders.

It is interesting that Jones and Nisbett's (1971) analysis of actor and observer may well apply to the leadership situation. Inevitably where trouble develops within an organization the character traits of the leader or leaders are usually blamed by observers of that situation, whereas the leaders themselves consistently put forward the idea that what they did was in response to their perception of the situation in which they found themselves.

As residential institutions vary from being small face-to-face groups in a living situation to huge complex organizations like prisons, it is inevitable that the whole gamut of ideas about leadership is applicable. Many of these ideas from research and recorded experience are already widely available in works on groups and on management, so this chapter will concentrate on filling some of the probable gaps in the literature as far as information is available.

For instance, though some form of co-leadership is familiar enough in all forms of small-group work, the salient evidence for its use is relatively hard to come by except for some specific forms. Yet many venturing into working with groups for the first time use a form of co-leadership as a kind of mutual support system in which the roles of an effective leader are shared by separate people, a true division of labour. At the other end of the scale there are management teams also exercising a form of division of labour often combined with a hierarchy of responsibility – what happens to the loyalty, dependence, and trust that gravitate to the leader of a small group in these circumstances? Is the response likely to be a constellation of small groups within the organization? And if so, what are the factors, if any, that bind this constellation into a confederation with at least some common aims?

Somewhere between these two forms, and perhaps related to the middle size of organization, is a form of leadership that could be called multiple leadership, where the status hierarchy is very flat and the power difference very small. Is it better to look at this as an extension of co-leadership where not two leaders but several occupy different but equal and (probably) interchangeable roles, or to see it as something completely different?

So much writing concerning leadership – that is, the act of leading – seems to be concerned with at most two co-operative leaders that long ago I abandoned the idea of leaders and concentrated on the performance of leadership acts. These are defined as those behaviours performed by any member of the group that are specifically produced in order to influence the behaviour of the group as a unit, or of any particular part of it. It is probably correct to assume that there has to be a degree of

conscious intent in the production of these events, but it is possible that the outcomes of such acts are not necessarily wholly in
line with the intent of the intervening member. He or she may
know that something needs to be done but may not be equally
aware of how it can be achieved.

In this case what I have called multiple leadership is a fact of
everyday life, and what perhaps makes it more interesting is that
instead of occurring between equals, i.e. the totality of the
group, it occurs between people at an equal level of status somewhere in the hierarchy of a middle-sized organization. Must we
suppose that multiple leadership produces a degree of efficiency,
i.e. achieves the aims of the system, in some kinds of organization more easily than other forms of leadership? In the course
of this chapter I will attempt to discuss some of these forms and
their relationship to group living.

One of the main areas of recent study in leadership has been
into the effects of different styles of leadership upon the functioning of the group. In 1973 Greening discussed the rejection
of the therapist's role by members of his group. He came to the
conclusion that trust and openness could be created in groups:

> 'The leader, however, must be willing to serve as a role model
> and active initiator rather than only a therapeutic facilitator.
> More importantly he must be prepared to help the group
> members make constructive use of their distrust and hostility
> toward him, and of their independent, anti-leader culture.'
> (Greening 1973: 248)

This is an example of the 'setting-the-standard' idea, which will
occur again in relation to co-leaders later in this chapter. When
people find themselves in an unfamiliar situation they tend to
look for examples of acceptable and safe ways of behaving. The
leader's function as a role model crucially affects what examples
are used. The difficulty is that discrepancies between verbal
clues as to what behaviour is acceptable and behavioural clues
usually compel members to accept the latter on the assumption
that they are more difficult to falsify. Greening suggests that
leaders should initiate behaviour that positively demonstrates
patterns of response and of coping which will eventually move

the group towards achieving its goals, including showing that hostility can be used productively.

Other researchers have tried to isolate the effects of leadership style on the interaction and satisfaction of group members. For instance, Gilstein, Wright, and Stone (1977) reported that they had found non-directive leaders to create more interaction within a group, and that the interaction was 'member-centred, work-response type'. In this case directive leadership was defined by the following behaviours:

(1) Leads the group verbally in discussion.
(2) Challenges members.
(3) Confronts members.
(4) Exhorts members.
(5) Suggests procedures for the group or for a member.
(6) Evaluates or interprets a response by a member.

Non-directive leadership was characterized by the following:

(1) Reflects feelings of members.
(2) Gives support, praise, or encouragement to members.
(3) Invites members to seek feedback.
(4) Summarizes what has been said.
(5) Allows group members to take responsibility for leading the group discussion.

I would suggest that, as the groups that were used to collect the data ran for six weeks at one hour and a half per session, which is not usually long enough for members of a group to develop a basic trust, there were other factors here that predisposed these groups to respond to non-directive leadership so quickly. Such leadership is most effective when a group has sorted out some of its basic socio-emotional problems and is able to work. Shaw and Blum (1966) thought that directive leadership was more effective than non-directive leadership only when leader/member relationships were good, when the group task was highly structured, and when the power and position of the leader were strong. Where these conditions did not prevail, then non-directive leadership was more effective.

Several studies have shown that where groups are engaged with a clear-cut task their members are task-oriented, less aggressive, and more involved than members of groups with ambiguous tasks. If these two factors are put together then it should be possible to discover which kind of leadership works best with what kind of task, and at what stage. Jurma (1978) found that group members, having completed a complex task, relate the value and interest they derived from it to the behaviour of the group leader. In unstructured tasks group members appear to rate highly the directive leader, but when tasks are clear-cut then directive and non-directive leaders are regarded as fairly similar. Directive leaders 'can increase group member morale by decreasing perceptions of failure' (Jurma 1978: 133).

So the old groupwork idea, that a clear task, a knowledge of the resources possessed by the group members, and good leader/member relationships with a given short period of time to produce an end result required a firm directive leadership, is shown to have research backing.

The effectiveness of leader behaviour is clearly related to the perceptions groups have of him or her. Shapiro and Klein (1975) showed that members' perceptions of leaders in encounter groups were

(1) highly inaccurate;
(2) more dissimilar at the beginning of a group and more similar later than the leaders actually were;
(3) more different from themselves at all stages of the group;
(4) distorted in a socially desirable direction.

Shapiro and Klein say that members' perceptions of leaders 'are contaminated by members' needs, wishes and fears' (see p. 137 on expectations). Thus effects achieved by group leaders may owe as much to what group members perceive to be the characteristics of group leaders as to the leaders' actual skill. Nydegger points out that 'in many instances it is not who the leader is, but rather what he does to meet certain needs of the group, that is significant' (1975: 364). He or she is the person who in return for influence, status, and esteem provides rewards for others in the form of fulfilling expectations and in achieving goals.

Reinforcement for agreeing with a member produces a better feeling towards that member than reinforcement for disagreeing with him or her, but good leaders maintain a favourable balance between rewards and costs.

In a rather limited study Weinstein and Hanson (1975) found that leaders with more experience were more consistent than those with less experience in:

(1) The amount of behaviour they initiated.
(2) Playing more complementary roles.
(3) Being treated more as a unit (where several leaders existed).
(4) Interacting more with each other.
(5) Having more influence on the range of group interactions.
(6) Having a lower received/initiate ratio (verbal exchanges).
(7) Having fewer silences.

Most of the foregoing serves to point up the fact that leadership behaviour that appears superficially as a relatively simple and easily definable pattern of behaviour is in reality very complex. Effects that in the past have been directly attributed to simple factors like personality and situation can now be seen to be the result of an amazing number of difficult-to-isolate factors. This makes the whole business of skill-training for leadership that much more crucial with every effort being made to ensure that potential leaders are aware of the interacting systems that will produce the consequences of leadership acts.

One way in which awareness of the multi-causal nature of these consequences can be developed is through the interchange of perceptions of co-leaders, and to this particular leadership phenomenon we must now turn.

CO-LEADERSHIP

In working with groups the concept of co-leadership has never received the attention it deserves. Many people have worked with colleagues in leadership roles and discovered for themselves the advantages and problems connected with such a procedure, and this will be considered below and will be concerned with direct work with groups within the residential system. What we are concerned with here is what information is available about co-leadership and about various forms of multiple leadership that would be useful to those working in residential institutions.

If the concept of 'leadership acts' mentioned earlier is brought to bear, co-leaders are in effect two or more members of a given group who carry out the role of leader rather more often than other members. They may also be, and often are, appointed as leaders. This may seem a semantic quibble, but it is not. Especially in the area we are considering, i.e. group living, some people are appointed by authority outside the group itself to be the leaders of that group, to have some power over its procedures and some concern for its welfare. They are designated leaders. Within any group there are those who, apart from the designated leaders, produce more leadership acts than other members. They have been called 'natural' leaders. It is a distinction that in reality draws attention to the different foundations of power upon which rests the exercise of leadership acts, and in most cases to the different areas of concern within an organization over which this power is exercised.

'Co-leaders' usually implies two people working together with a group. One way of looking at this is to see the two (dyad) as a sub-group within the group, a sub-group that has the special role of being leaders. Much has been written about this dyad; e.g. it promotes security (Slavson 1953), it increases the efficacy of treatment (Rosenbaum 1971), it creates a unique opportunity for personal and professional growth to be made available to the therapist (Block 1961). Dies, Mallet, and Johnson (1979) have suggested that co-leadership can provide:

(1) Enhanced perception of group and individual dynamics.
(2) Enhanced ability to resolve therapeutic impasses.
(3) Increased opportunities for modelling.
(4) Greater potential for useful feedback to the leaders.

As can be seen, most of the material about co-leadership comes from therapeutic and encounter groups and their facilitators, so some care must be taken, and the findings should not be accepted without reservations. But role-modelling a relationship that works — adults who can agree with one another, a relationship of male/female that functions and can cope with difference — is clearly one of the main virtues. Such a relationship has to be based upon an accord between the leaders, a clear understanding of the roles each will play within the group sessions, good preparation beforehand, and exhaustive feedback and recording afterwards so that the partnership really does work.

Dies, Mallet, and Johnson (1979) noted that an enhanced perception of dynamics was a bonus of co-leadership. Two people regarding the same situation at the same time will see significantly different things, and if these are put together then blind spots and 'never-thought-of-that' areas can be diminished or at least brought into awareness.

Winter (1976) suggested that the co-leaders could use their partnership to demonstrate to the group how the problems of each phase of group development (see p. 67) might be met and resolved. For instance, they could show in the early stages of a group that trust and working together are possible, the group at this stage having to cope with exactly the problem of gaining sufficient experience of each other to develop enough trust to be able to work together. Co-leaders can demonstrate conflict that does not destroy, the fact of being together yet being different, and how to gain maximum benefit from each other's experience at the end of a group.

Security has been mentioned briefly as a reason for working with a co-leader, something akin to a dyadic support system being developed. Group leading can be very frightening, and the presence of another to share what goes on can often be an anxiety-relieving system. When one leader is more experienced than another this can create an on-the-spot learning situation that can be very valuable provided it does not become a straightforward imitation procedure.

We said at the beginning of this section that co-leadership was a dyadic group. Sometimes the dyad becomes an even bigger group and there is a form of multiple leadership, in fact a team. For very large groups this may well be an effective form of leadership. For instance, in a large youth club four people acted as leaders. When they became organized they allocated roles for each leader throughout the session, conferred at given points throughout it, and discussed the whole process when it was over. They found this added a great deal of richness to what they were able to observe and to what they were able to control or initiate. For the first time they were able to see the transient and permanent groupings, the ebb and flow of members, to detect sequences leading to the generation of interest, excitement, boredom, and disruption. Their shared vision, the parts put together, gave a much clearer picture of a complex set of interactions and reduced the possibility that their ignorance of parts of what was happening could be used to play one leader off against the others.

One problem arises with multiple leadership relating to the power ratio. If a group is small with several designated leaders, then the power ratio is seen to be threatening to the members and is unlikely to allow them to feel able to relax into the group's behaviour. This is a situation often found in large ward meetings in some psychiatric hospitals.

Much of what has been said so far has greater application to designated leaders, but, as I said earlier, leadership acts rather than leaders are what influences group behaviour. For this reason we must now look at what has been called 'peer leadership', leadership acts made by members of a group who have no designated leader status. Until fairly recently such groups were often referred to as 'leaderless', which is a misnomer because all groups contain potential leaders; the term was also markedly condescending, suggesting that groups without a designated leader were 'leaderless' even though the implications of equality and democracy were the basis for the description.

PEER LEADERSHIP

Cattell (1951) defined a leader as 'a person who produces a group syntality[1] different from that which would have existed had he not been present in the group, and his leadership ability is measured by the magnitude of the changes he produces along all dimensions of the syntality'. As Bednarek, Benson, and

Mustafa (1976) say, this means that every group member is in some degree a leader. Thus we come to the concept of peer leadership.

Group members differ widely in their ability to influence the group. In any case, the way the group accepts or rejects influence attempts may well be the major factor in who emerges, and for how long, as a peer leader. But some research has shown that group members seem to be able to predict those of their fellows who will emerge as leaders with a considerable degree of accuracy. Schultz (1978) asked group members to rate each other on a seven-point scale of nineteen variables. After the group had been in existence for some time she asked them to say what leaders had emerged. Using only three of the nineteen variables, Schultz was able to predict after the first session eleven of the fifteen emerging leaders. The three variables that were so remarkably accurate in predicting which members would emerge as leaders were:

(1) An ability to formulate goals for the group.
(2) An ability to summarize group proceedings.
(3) An ability to give directions to the group.

Bednarek, Benson, and Mustafa (1976) also investigated how leaders were selected in a group of peers. They discovered that when the group was performing a task that was functional and technical, then the group tended to opt for leaders from among their numbers who were most knowledgeable or at least were perceived to be so. When the task involved interpersonal relationships, then the leader chosen would be one the members believed they could confide in. It is common sense, of course, to pick the most useful person in each case, and this squares with French and Raven's (1959) idea of awarding power to people perceived to possess useful specialist skills and knowledge.

Bednarek, Benson, and Mustafa eventually isolated four factors that they considered would be sufficient for group members to identify potential leaders. They were:

(1) Task factor – defined by knowledge, judgement, dominance, responsibility, ambition, influence, co-operation, being the preferred co-worker, self-assuredness.

(2) Maturity factor – defined by the personality traits of emotional control, extraversion, conviction, co-operation, and judgement.
(3) Social influence – defined by friendship and informal leadership.
(4) Flexibility or adaptability – defined by the ability to 'get along' with others, a willingness to co-operate with the peer group.

Given the fact that the groups Bednarek and colleagues were examining were work groups in an office, these factors define the kinds of attribute a leader would need to emerge in such a group. It is clear also that choice of leader resides just as much in the kind of task the group is concerned with as in the perceived attributes that may be available.

Like co-leadership, peer leadership has never been well investigated, and so the material we have is very much what common sense would have led us to believe anyway. This lack of research data is surprising in view of the fact that self-help groups are essentially peer-led groups and they have been promoted in many social contexts for a very long time. It is also remarkable that groupworkers seeking to achieve groups in which the members understand and can use the processes of their own groups for the attainment of their goals are essentially concerned with achieving peer-led groups. It may be that the concept of 'peer-led' is new; it may be that ideas about democratic groups have masked the real leadership behaviour of such groups; but the fact remains that, apart from descriptive studies of self-help groups, the way in which such groups are led and on what basis leaders are chosen have attracted little research data. It may also be concerned with the apparent dislike of the idea of leadership and the use of power that is still widely prevalent amongst people working with groups, as witness the aversion often expressed to directive forms of leadership. Yet what often prevails in groups is not the overt direction of a controlling leader, but a manipulative leadership, which appears on the surface to be wholly permissive but is not. Such a leadership is indeed very skilful, but it has no need to be hidden behind a mask of apparent non-directiveness, but openly accepted for what it is.

All leadership requires the commitment of energy to the group: to get it started, to help it move in the direction it needs to move in, to hold it together by providing sufficient satisfactions to maintain interest, to act as a resource, guide, and arbiter, to help when help is needed, to be a focal point for hostility, affection, resentment, and challenges for power, to be the terminator, evaluator, and eventually the generator of understanding.

As leadership is open to all members of a group it is necessary that they should have some idea about what that commitment of energy is all about and how it can be wasted or transformed into beneficial products for the group.

LEADERSHIP AND THE CONCEPT OF THE GROUP AS AN ENERGY TRANSFORMATION SYSTEM

To regard a group as an energy system seems to provide a good basis for understanding certain kinds of leadership behaviour. However, it must be recognized from the outset that a group of human beings poses certain problems when regarded as such a system.

'Social systems, however, are not anchored in the same physical constancies as biological organisms and so are capable of almost indefinite arresting of the entropic process.'
(Katz and Kahn 1969: 95)

By implication people have the ability to assess what is happening within a system and to make a conscious decision to commit more or less energy to it on the basis of a purely personal perception. The entropic process of running down may then be accelerated or arrested as a function of conscious decisions; this constitutes an essential piece of knowledge for all those who work with groups and is equally valid for those who become members of groups.

In the initial stages of a group's development it is true to say that a few people, sometimes only one, have an overall perception of the ultimate value that the forming group might have for its members. At this stage the energy commitment of the members is at best cautious at worst may be resistive. If the energy component drops far enough the group will not work; if the work that is required to generate interest and therefore commitment of energy is too great it will reduce the level of satisfaction, and a 'double bind' or even a 'can't win' syndrome will appear to develop.

What exactly is meant by 'energy' in the case of groups? There are in fact two major kinds: one that is truly external to the group, usually a supportive influence coming from the larger system of which the group is a part; and one that is the energy from the group members. Let us take the second one first as it may prove the more difficult to deal with.

The energy that members commit to a group is compounded of many factors – interest, self-preservation, perception of value or worth, curiosity, desperation, and so on; in fact, all those influences that will impel people to commit firstly time and secondly effort to attending the group. Why put such an emphasis on attending? To attend means that at least inertia has been overcome, so energy has been involved, and a cost/reward balance for the individual has shifted to allow that energy to be expended. It is amazing how distance and difficulty of travelling seem to become insuperable problems for group members only when the satisfaction they obtain from attending diminishes or fails to occur. This diminution may take place, for many reasons, but its overall effect on the group when absence occurs is to diminish the attenders' satisfaction also: a kind of knock-on effect that requires an increment of satisfaction to be added to the group if possible to halt the process.

When people join treatment groups they are often at a very low ebb, and virtually any form of human activity could be regarded as a plus. Then the potential satisfaction to be gained from being a member of a group is very great because of starting from such a long way down. However, when attendance at a group has produced an uplift, then the balance between the costs of attending and the satisfactions starts to level out. If the costs overtake the rewards then that member will opt out of the group unless he or she is able to anticipate future rewards that will compensate for current costs.

Energy, then, is commitment to the group. But it is also the effort of working as a member, contributing skills, knowledge, sympathy, affection, resources, and above all sharing. The problem is that life experience may have taught most people that they have to be cautious, so any energy that may be available at the beginning of a group may well be tentative or misdirected.

As we have seen, any system consumes energy just to maintain itself in existence. In the early stages of a group the work committed to the group by the leader or leaders has therefore to be relatively high. They are almost compelled to accept a future reward for current energy costs. That reward will be of a group able to supply its own energy needs because commitment is high, since what the group has to offer its members is a high level of satisfaction. The leader has to create from discrete individuals a functioning unit providing a good margin of rewards over costs for those individuals and him- or herself.

This need for energy from a particular source, i.e. the leader, may not be restricted to the early stages of a group's formation, but can also occur at times during its life when crisis has caused a diminution of reward. Of course this might be terminal, but if the leader or any other group member has a belief that the group can be assisted to provide more satisfaction in the future, then he or she will probably make a judgement that the commitment necessary to keep it going may be worthwhile. When groups complete the task(s) for which they were established then energy is withdrawn and diverted elsewhere so that the group closes.

The other form of energy, which was described as being external to the group, tends to reside in the support and encouragement it receives from other than its own membership. Large organizations can soon create conditions in which groups can proliferate and thrive. Equally they can squeeze unwanted groups out of existence. The squeezing process is not always successful depending on the stage of development of the group; it may serve to make it bind much more closely together. Such organizations can also create a situation in which groups can easily start and in which their achievements are strictly limited.

Thus external energy comes from an encouraging atmosphere, being given space to move, to create, being accorded material and financial help, administrative assistance, accommodation, etc. – all tending to create a milieu that helps by not diverting energy from the group into fighting and attempting to change adverse conditions. Some outside help is positive; in some cases it is just not contrary.

When the leader(s) has to produce a large input of energy at the start of a group, the process is usually described as 'holding', i.e. keeping the group together long enough for some of the rewards it can offer its members to become manifest. It is a delicate operation, simply because too much of the wrong kind of energy producing a good level of satisfaction for members can also cause a dependence upon the state that will exactly prevent the development of the group and eventually exhaust the ideas, interests, people, and places that the leader can offer.

It is necessary also to explain the word 'transformation'. In this case it means that the work members put into the group creates a product in some senses in roughly the same way that a factory translates or transforms raw materials into a finished product through the application of energy through labour and machine processes. The product for the group equates with some form of change. In a problem-solving group the change is from problem to solution; in a personal-growth group the change is in the generation of personal insight; in a therapeutic group the change is in the modification of behavioural patterns, and so on.

The fundamental point about leader behaviour in this context is that it has to be the agent by which the possibility of the transformation of energy into desired and desirable change can take place. Often enough this form of leader behaviour is called 'directive' largely because the leader is assumed to be a person who, having trodden this path before, is better able to set his or her current group members in the right direction and to hold them together until they become sure of it. There is nothing intrinsically at fault in being directive; only when such behaviour does not relate to the needs of the group does it become an ego-trip on the part of the leader and damaging to the development of the group.

GROUPWORK IN A GROUP-LIVING SITUATION

Much of this book is concerned with beginning to understand how residential organizations operate using the information available about group behaviour. But it is not feasible to ignore the fact that within residential settings groups may be created for specific purposes, thus establishing in a conscious way a sub-system or systems within the larger organization (see p. 158 on embedding, and p. 60 on sub-groups). Such sub-systems tend to condense around specific tasks, actions, or aims, and even groups that are self-creating on the basis of friendship also have a powerful focal interest in such matters as security.

To 'create' a group does not necessarily mean that separate individuals are deliberately brought together with conscious intent, though I am aware that this is the way most people think when groupwork is mentioned. It is equally valid to take an existing group formed for whatever purpose and probably unaware of its unitary nature except to some limited extent, and work with it as a discrete entity. Perhaps a family would be a prime example of this kind of pre-existing group: completely aware of the bonding that exists and of special relationships, but not usually accustomed to regarding itself with clarity as a group, nor wholly aware of the dynamics of its group inter-action.

If for the moment we ignore self-created groups, which we have already looked at (p. 60 on sub-groups), and concentrate on those groups that are deliberately condensed out of a larger resident public, we need to note several facts.

The first is that any group specifically created within a larger group organization has to create boundaries for itself, and by so doing it also creates highly visible divisions of the included and the excluded. This division exists for all groups and is always emphasized by a clash of loyalty between two groups where one person is a member of both. But in the general world of groups the visibility of membership/non-membership is slight; in residential settings it is often very great. This is particularly so if membership of a certain group is deemed to be eminently desirable, because this then generates an élite. The reality of élite status is enhanced by the 'reporting' syndrome, whereby those who have experienced a situation that others of the larger organization have not tend to report it in such a way that adds increments of stature, of superiority, of difference to those having undergone the experience. This does not apply just to groups but to individual experiences as well; e.g. students having successfully survived certain kinds of course create a mystique about it that serves to enhance them as successful candidates.

The establishment of élites within a residential setting can cut across other group boundaries and create jealousies and ill-feeling. Equally it can have a positive effect, especially with a system that makes it possible for all members to experience most things on offer. In some organizations, where new entrants are stripped down to the lowest point of tolerable self-esteem, the programme of progress is based upon the need to achieve. Thus each stage of the resident's progress is to move to a group with higher status than his or her last till in the end he or she may become one of the select group putting others through the whole process. The purpose of the élite here is to offer an attainable target towards which even the lowest may aspire. Far from casting doubts on whether one is 'chosen' or 'not chosen' by the powers that be, it encourages achievement through incremental rewards of self-esteem, status, and power.

Another major difference for specifically created groups within a residential setting is the effect of embedding, which will be dealt with in greater detail (p. 158). It must suffice here to say that the seepage of influence across all group boundaries within a large organization is immediate, powerful, and ultimately very constraining. This is not necessarily bad; indeed, it may well be of enormous value to any group, provided that the group's aims and procedures are within the range of tolerance of deviance that the organization is prepared to allow. The larger the organization, the poorer its communication system tends to be and the less likely it will be to discover deviant groups quickly unless it has a system specifically designed to do just that. There is an old maxim often heard in very large organizations that if a group and its ideas are unheard of then it must be harmless. While there is some truth in this, insidious small-group activity has ultimately destroyed or changed very large organizations.

If a group is set up within a larger organization, then the purposes for which it is established and the methods by which they will be pursued must be compatible with the declared aims of the larger body unless it is set up deliberately to effect change in that organization. A major point here is that the compatibility may have to be not just with the aims of the organization as a whole, but also with those of the major powerful sub-groups within it. For instance, the governor of a closed institution, having experienced the effects of working with groups of lads in his previous post, attempted to establish a groupwork system within his new institution. He instigated courses for staff and discussions for all involved and set up a comprehensive programme. Within months he knew that he had failed for the simple reason that a large and powerful sub-group within the organization had decided that groupwork was not the kind of approach for which they deemed the institution had been established. As groupwork is extremely susceptible to being undermined in a residential setting, this was what happened. No open hostility to the idea was expressed, but various parts of its organization and performance were effectively sabotaged and its usefulness was diminished until even the governor had to admit that it was not working and revert to the previous system.

Another effect of working with a group in a residential setting, especially one with no basic design pattern of groupwork, is that of splitting off various parts of the overall residential task into the care of specialists. Often enough this can deprive full-time staff of some of the more interesting parts of their role with a consequent loss of job satisfaction and withdrawal of commitment.

Ultimately the use of specifically created groups offers to residents extra experience over and above what is generally available. The contagion effect may well be instrumental in spreading some of the effects of this experiential learning, provided the negative counter-effects of jealousy can be controlled. Groups can be used to create learning situations related to special need, to acquire and practise new and necessary skills. But what must always be remembered is that for whatever process they are created they are not isolate units in their own right. What will be said many times in the course of this book is that however much or little a groupworker may take into consideration the effects of the larger system in which his or her groups are embedded, he or she may rest assured that its effects will manifest themselves in any case.

I think it appropriate to end this section with some comments by Cartwright (1966) on the principles governing the group as a medium of change. He listed five:

(1) That the 'changers' and those to be changed need to have a strong sense of belonging to the same group.
(2) The more attractive a group is to its members the greater the influence it can exert.
(3) If the relevance of the attitudes, values, and behaviour that form the basis of attraction to the group is great, the greater the influence the group can exert upon them.
(4) The more prestige a member has within the group the greater his or her influence.
(5) Any effort to change an individual member or sub-group that causes them to deviate from the norms of the group will meet strong resistance.

Cartwright went on to say that strong influence for change can be brought about if the group creates a shared perception of the need for change. This kind of influence needs to be supported by information relating to the need for, plans for, and consequences of change, which must be shared by all. Cartwright further pointed out that change in one part of a group inevitably produces strain and tension in other related parts, which can be reduced only by stopping the initial change taking place or by setting up adaptive patterns of adjustment in the stressed parts.

Working with a group within a residential setting it is essential to remember that the position of the group *vis-à-vis* the larger organization of which it is part is often very similar to that of the individual member or sub-group to the group. Thus the 'change' nature of groups referred to by Cartwright has to be seen in relationship not just to the working group but also to the institution of which it is part – a double responsibility. It is not surprising that change is not so easy to come by in residential settings when so many of the factors listed above are limited by the very structural organization of that setting.

WORKING WITH RESIDENTIAL GROUPS

This chapter may be said to contain the most easily accessible ideas about the interrelated nature of the dynamics of group behaviour. The leader is an individual in whom focuses all the experience, knowledge, and skill of his or her past; co-leaders are dyads, the smallest group; multiple leadership produces a group (team) leading other groups within an organization; and peer leadership shows evidence that all group members can make leadership acts. This is not an absolutely clear progression, granted, but one that serves to demonstrate how all systems contain smaller systems and are contained within larger systems, and indeed how apparently simple behaviour patterns can stem from very complex causes.

How does what has been said so far relate to residential systems? The simple answer is that in all such systems leadership of many kinds is practised and that any information which might serve to enlighten that practice or inform it is to be thought of as valuable.

The first point to make is that within any group-living situation there are leaders. Some are designated leaders, employed for their skills in creating specific living conditions for others, controlling, being responsible for management, organization, treatment, care, etc.; others are 'natural' leaders arising from within the client population. Whatever workers are taught within the group-living situation, most of the evidence (e.g. Millham, Bullock, and Hosie 1980) points to the unfortunate fact that leadership skills and a knowledge of the dynamics of groups do not figure very largely.

Part of this chapter has been devoted to showing that leadership itself must be seen in the context in which it occurs. Thus much of the material related to leadership of non-residential groups has to be modified when applied in group living. In non-residential groups, membership forms a small but significant part of a member's life; other parts of his or her life are passed under different environmental circumstances with different people. Contacts are different and can serve to place any group membership in a wide context of social living. The power of designated leaders resides in the skills and knowledge that facilitate the group's progress and in personality.

In the residential system there are marked differences to this situation. In very large systems there may be an opportunity to make contact with others, but the containing institution is the same; group membership here is always subsumed under the one system that forms the context for the evaluation of such membership. Designated leaders are not just leaders of groups; they also hold positions of some authority within the containing institution and are frequently contacted in different roles outside any particular group situation. These containing factors facilitate an immediate spread of knowledge about people involved in a group in terms of their behaviour, attitudes, opinions, and beliefs as displayed in the confined and related other areas of the same system.

As this chapter has shown, members' perceptions of group leaders, though better than their perceptions of each other, are not very accurate in ordinary groups. In residential groups such perceptions are liable to be much more widely based because of the increased area of contact. Therefore members' expectations are founded on a different base to those occurring in non-residential groups.

The capacity of leaders to act as a role model cannot be restricted to the behaviour produced within a special group context. This kind of effect is noted earlier in terms of the restricting effect that environmental factors have on the leader's ability to influence the group. There is a much greater difficulty in a group-living situation in adopting a particular leadership style for a particular group within the system because it immediately has to bear comparison with that person's behaviour elsewhere in the system, which is known about, and differences can be perceived in this case as deception.

In the discussion on co-leaders one of the research findings was that openness between the leaders and between leaders and the group paid big dividends in the personal growth of the group members. Caution was expressed that this might not be true about non-therapeutic groups. I would hazard a guess that such openness is not only good but a prerequisite of existence in a group-living situation where the kind of observable discrepancies in leader behaviour can avoid the criticism of deceit only if they are owned by the people using them and openly discussed, including the reasons for their use. Of course if discussion will not and cannot lead to modification if required then this also will be assessed as being a gambit that is consciously deceitful in nature.

The kind of leadership available within a group-living situation is in general much more firmly constrained by environmental factors than in groups in non-residential settings. The embedded nature of all groups within the residential scene is that much more obvious. Any group is a small part of a larger group; the same people form the membership of different groups; even the use of co-leadership produces a group of two with a special role within one group apart from any other sub-groupings that may form. The concept of the energy system is often masked in group-living situations because bodies are there because they 'live' there, and it is not attendance that is a significant marker of interest but rather the quality of that attendance and the energy invested in the group for or against – which are much more difficult criteria to establish.

Even when groups are used as instruments in their own right within the group-living system they are still contextually engaged with the larger system, and its influence may be a paramount factor in what they are able to achieve. For instance, goals within the group that are in contradiction to the policy of the larger organization may be found to be unobtainable and thus help in generating apathy amongst group members, or cause conflict and disruption. All groups can tolerate subgroups where the goals are different from those of the containing group, but that difference cannot be too great; in some kinds of organization the tolerance of difference is in fact very small unless the difference in itself demonstrably produces rewards for the larger group. These rewards may be energy, initiative, new ideas, greater production, success with groups outside the organization, and so on. As the researchers say, difference is tolerated only in so far as either it does not matter and can be contained or it is produced by members of high status within the organization who can produce rewards for it.

The ultimate aim of some group leaders is to create a situation in which their group members begin to understand the dynamics of group behaviour and become able to use this knowledge to further the group's and their own ends. In some group-living situations such self-directing behaviour may never be a real possibility, but there is much evidence to indicate that to have even a little control over the decisions affecting one's life is better than to have none at all. Peer leadership is thus a way of ensuring that group members do seek to influence their group, know how to do it, and are helped to achieve that level of power consonant with their abilities and the constraints of the system.

In essence the whole of this chapter is to be regarded as a set of signposts to what is involved in leadership behaviour in group-living situations. As usual the most important point is that of signalling the complex nature of such situations, which requires that a sensitivity to, and awareness of, what is going on should be developed in those working in residential systems. Even with no aspirations to groupwork skills, a knowledge of the energy systems and their influence is an absolute essential. Otherwise most of the causes of behavioural patterns in living groups will remain hidden and invisible, but nevertheless potent.

NOTE

1 Group syntality: the dimensions along which groups change, e.g. integration, sociability, or trust.

6 Relationships

Next to leadership, the literature on groups probably contains more references to personal relationships and attraction than to anything else. Within the boundaries of a group, personal relationships, friendships, support systems, and liked and disliked member responses make a kaleidoscopic pattern of alliances, cliques, and groupings, which form, exist, and then break and form again sometimes with different members. People leave, new people arrive, and affections change. The stabilities and fluidities of these situations greatly affect what a group can achieve; and while the more obvious hostilities and affections can be seen easily enough for what they are and their effects monitored, this is not so for the less obvious relationships.

Patterns of relationship have a tight correlation with the structure of the group (see Chapter 3). As we shall see at the start of Chapter 7, a structure of management founded upon the special relationship of all members to the leader poses dependency problems similar to that of the keystone of an arch; when this is removed, what was a firm and effective structure collapses unless some other structure has been created to hold it in place.

'Relationship' is a term with wide connotations. In the first instance relationships have to be with people, animals, or things; it is hardly possible to talk about relationships in the abstract. But like most factors relating to groups relationships form a seen and unseen network of more or less meaningful connections among the members and between the members and others who are not members. Once more we are faced with recognizing the existence of endless possibilities that can affect what goes on in the group, and once more we are compelled to choose those kinds of relationship pattern from this mass that appear to have the greatest effect upon group behaviour.

For that reason this chapter, though short, will look at some of the information that promises to be of most value about interpersonal attraction (the relationship of liking), about expectations (the set of assumptions group members have about the possible relationships they will have from and with other members), about the fundamental factors of acceptance and rejection, again both by others and of others, about what kind of relationship may be implied by being made or becoming an isolate within the group, and about that special relationship often described as 'friendship'. As in everything else connected with human behaviour and interaction, idiosyncratic perception complicates the picture. Thus *A*'s perception that *B* likes him will condition *A*'s response to *B* as if this was an accepted fact, whereas it may well be an assumption that does not accurately correspond with *B*'s perception of his feelings for *A*. The further complication is what is discussed under expectations when the position between *A* and *B* is as last described but *B* has an expectation that his perception of his lack of liking for *A* must on no account be permitted to show because of the response it may entail from *A* and from other group members as well and even from *B* himself in terms of his expectations of himself. Further, whatever relationships exist between members of a group, relationship-making and -breaking behaviour – sometimes called 'attachment' behaviour – is a process and is not the relationship itself.

At the end of the chapter the ways in which these matters concerning relationships might affect the group-living situation are discussed. Although most people are astonished when they realize that the number and the nature of relationships they can make with others are constrained by opportunity, and that in many cases this works out at a surprisingly small overall number over a given period of time, residential institutions highlight this matter of restricted choice very well. The number of possible relationships is often quite clearly displayed, and this restricted choice may be reduced even further by lack of interest in, and dislike of, what is available.

Lack of choice in relationships may not precipitate a complete withdrawal but it does usually mean a restriction of the basis upon which a relationship may be made in terms of its nature and quality, its transient or permanent state, and the degree of involvement. An isolate may be one who rejects any closer involvement with the group, so that his or her position is self-chosen. It may also be imposed in that the group have ostracized him or her. The reasons for ostracism are many but nearly always contain some element of either dislike or lack of conformity to group norms.

Another point highlighted by residential systems is that when a system comprises two major sub-groups, the processors and the processed, an extra dimension of relationships has to be considered. This is especially so when part of the skill training of one sub-group, the processors, contains a large element of deliberate relationship creation and use as part of its work. There is no doubt that conscious attachment-seeking behaviour is a part of everyday social intercourse, but its ends are essentially selfish and personal. Conscious relationship formation, which has benefit for the object of the relationship as its end and is part of some form of therapeutic endeavour, is an extremely different animal and is one main reason why the charge of artificiality is frequently levelled at it. But then there is the argument that residential systems are themselves artificial creations and substitutes for 'naturally' occurring systems that have proved ineffective. Thus the system and maybe the relationships to be found within it are seen as taking on the same nature.

INTERPERSONAL ATTRACTION

In a scan of the literature on interpersonal attraction Raven and Rubin listed seven determinants of liking another, namely:

'their personal characteristics or traits, a feeling of unity or identification with them, their liking for us, the fact that they offer us some material benefits, the fact that we feel comfortable with them, justification of our efforts on their behalf (reduction of dissonance), and the fact they offer us a means of evaluating ourselves.'

(1976: 111)

These determinants were elicited about interpersonal attraction in ordinary everyday life, but in a group situation, in particular a residential group, their relevance is even greater. If we take these seven factors in turn, this can be demonstrated.

(1) Personal characteristics or traits

In the world at large the personal characteristics of those we meet may appear attractive or not, but in the confines of a residential situation personal traits can seem to become exaggerated. Physical appearance has often been quoted as one of the main reasons why we like others; certainly there is some evidence to indicate that those whose physical appearance fits the standards of the observer are treated differently to those who do not fit, whatever their merits may be. Sudnow, for example, noted that doctors were much less eager to pronounce a casualty 'dead on arrival' if 'the patient was younger, well-to-do, nicely dressed, clean and without the smell of alcohol — generally of pleasing appearance' (1967: 114).

Personal appearance is perhaps the most obvious of personal characteristics, but habits like personal cleanliness, which are often equally visible to only a small number of people, become much more intrusive and to larger numbers when people are collected together and compelled to live a large part of their lives, for a period of time at least, in unchosen companionship. Many times when people find themselves in this sort of situation they are confronted with the realization that the very characteristics which made them liked in other situations do nothing to gain the liking of their current companions. Behaviour traits that are likeable and quaint in other situations come to be regarded as irritating and stupid when there is little possibility of being able to diminish the effect of these traits by withdrawal.

Liking in group situations tends to be based on those personal characteristics that adapt well to over-exposure, relate positively to the situation, and have an element of reassurance rather than threat about them. Of course liking is still a highly personal matter, though group membership can modify the individual perception of what is likeable.

(2) Unity and/or identification

One factor that runs throughout this analysis of personal attraction is similarity. Thus unity or identification with others is based on the perception of similarity: membership of the same social class; possession of the same status, same sex, social organization, race, or religion; holding similar beliefs or attitudes; possessing similar characteristics or experience; having common goals or aims; being subject to the same form of threat.

It is not surprising that groups develop a sense of belonging (cohesion) and are able to work together only after the members have spent sufficient time together to become aware of what they have in common and of whether what they have not got in common is important to the task they are currently following. Identification does not have to be based in actual similarity; it can be founded in the desire to emulate, but it is none the less potent for that. Being together in a group does provide shared experience, as those who have been through hardship and fear together know only too well. The bonds forged in those circumstances may be very long lasting even when the sharers never meet again after the event that brought them together. Equally they may withdraw from each other with great relief at the end of the crisis, the intense relationship having been a means to an end.

(3) The liking of others for us

It is not always so, but there is some evidence that we respond warmly to those who like us. Much depends upon our estimate of ourselves, our self-esteem, and upon the perception we have of the motives for the expression of liking. I have seen time and again in groups members respond to the expression of liking with surprise and later gratitude. Our society is notorious for its acceptance that criticism is normal but that praise and the expression of affection are not. People have to guess from indirect clues whether others like them or not, and the resultant element of uncertainty can be very stressful. It is possible that a direct statement of liking may be a gambit in a deceitful game, but at least it is an expression of interest. The general suspiciousness generated within our society is a major factor in isolating individuals from affection, so an expression of liking may well produce a relief-oriented response of liking in return.

(4) Material benefits

Although a cost/reward analysis of a relationship may seem somewhat calculating, there is no doubt that some element of accounting enters into personal attraction. Such a simple statement must immediately be hedged with qualifications because we have no way of knowing what satisfactions an individual may derive from a relationship nor what weight they may give to them. When people stay in a relationship that appears destructive and harmful, it can only be assumed that through a personal and individual assessment of the situation they have discovered beneficial factors that are hidden to others and outweigh the obvious disadvantages. Social exchange theory asserts that we give in order to get and that costs and rewards *are* carefully assessed.

(5) Feelings of comfort with others

Familiarity tends to be based upon predictability, which tends to generate security or at least a reduced expectation of surprise. But familiarity itself arises only over a long period of time and contact. In the residential setting where contact with a limited population almost serves to define the situation, familiarity can be controlled only by withdrawal, i.e. by reducing the intensity of otherwise unavoidable contact.

(6) Justification of our efforts

Apparently the harder the effort we have to make to enter and maintain our membership of a group, the greater we appear to like what we eventually achieve. The corollary of this is that what is easily come by is little regarded.

(7) Help in self-evaluation

There is some evidence that we like those who share our predicament of having to re-evaluate ourselves. Much of this evidence comes from therapy and personal-growth groups and it is seen to be important only when survival and growth are at stake.

It should be evident from the foregoing brief look at inter-personal attraction that an apparently simple social phenom-enon can be complex to understand. In Schutz's (1959) thesis of the developmental pattern of groups he placed affection – that is, liking – as the third and last of the stages that group mem-bers reach in establishing a working group. Even so, having reached a level of liking that enabled the group to function he believed that the process was being continually repeated at levels of increasing sophistication in healthy groups as the members had more experience of each other in different situ-ations. When the group was coming to an end it became the first stage to be discharged.

EXPECTATIONS

Raven and Rubin, discussing the 'expectancy effect' in exper-imental studies, wrote:

> 'when subjects are brought to an experimental laboratory (an unfamiliar, peculiar and perhaps threatening environment), they rapidly come to the accurate conclusion that their behaviour is being observed and that they may be expected to perform in certain predictable ways.'

> (1976: 491)

The fact that this was an experimental situation was irrelevant. Everyone brings into all social situations expectations of what might ensue, so that any group anywhere at any time is a conflu-ence of the expectations of its members. Some of these expec-tations are in the process of being realized, and others are not; some are being modified to meet perceptions that have become changed in the course of membership; others are being rigidly adhered to in an attempt to make the situation as they see it conform to their expectations of it. Everyone has expectations about everyone and everything else, and the whole complex net-work of expectations forms one of the major issues governing commitment, satisfaction, involvement, and response in group situations.

Before exploring these factors one other point has to be made. In all group situations where one person — the leader, director, facilitator, or therapist — is deemed by the other group members to possess special qualities of either power or knowledge, then his or her expectations of the group will tend to influence its behaviour even though those expectations are never expressed (Rosenthal 1966, Rosenthal and Rosnow 1969).

In essence, expectations are a method of mental preparation for an event or situation that has not yet occurred but may well be about to do so. In some way expectations are engendered as a result of rehearsing in one's mind what may be in store and how best one might plan to use one's resources to cope with it. It may well be that much of this preparation for an event or situation that has not yet occurred is made without a great deal of attention being given to it, but the essential fact is that given any foreknowledge whatsoever we prepare. The anticipation of the form of the future event can be based only on assumption or knowledge; hence the saying 'familiarity breeds contempt' — there is little anxiety when event and expectation are assumed to be completely matched.

Where knowledge is not complete then assumptions based upon the information available must be made; and because of the uncertainty, anxiety about the outcome is a very likely companion. Where expectations are unrealistic, either because they contain an element of fantasy or because they are inaccurate, then problems occur. Either expectations are adjusted to meet the realities of the event that is here now, or the event is rejected as not being what was expected, or some element of confusion and uncertainty ensues. Perhaps the worst situation of the lot occurs when, for some reason or other, the evidence of the actual situation is not accepted, and the individual continues to hold expectations of a situation that are not consistent with its reality. The level of frustration and disappointment eventually experienced in this way is often very great.

Individuals become members of groups carrying with them unacknowledged expectations of the way that the group will function. No one has ever taught them that similarities are not necessarily or even usually exactly identical. So although no boundaries are set or rules given, behaviour that is strictly conforming with the expected patterns is produced. Is this a function of a security need or of a blindness to the possibility of choice? Is freedom to choose so frightening or is it that we are habituated to certain modes of behaviour and cannot recognize that the usual constraints are not there until someone tells us or gives us permission to see that they are not there?

Expectations that are not expressed but continue to influence not only what the individual contributes to the group but also what he or she sees happening there are often referred to as a 'hidden agenda'. Sometimes the 'hidden' means not revealed but known to the individual; i.e. he or she is pursuing undisclosed personal aims within the context of the group. But more often it means that the expectations are not wholly known to the individual holding them; they are carried-over business from previous similar experiences, habitual responses long forgotten but nevertheless active, or half-formed ideas about what is anticipated. In any case they are all powerful influences on response patterns, commitment, and satisfaction, and need to be taken into consideration. We may never truly know what they are in any given group, but we do know they exist because of the observable consequences of their influence.

Attempts to have expectations expressed are only as effective as the perceptions of the individual in indicating to him or her what degree of personal safety lies in disclosure. Such attempts are nevertheless the best method that can be devised of uncovering assumptions and of creating a pool of knowledge about motivation. But even here expectation rules. No one will disclose their assumptions about their expectations if among them is the expectation that it is unsafe to do so. Only when others have demonstrated that security exists will those expectations perhaps be modified. In this respect it is fortunate that both our expectations and our perceptions of what constitutes safety are different.

ACCEPTANCE AND REJECTION

Wilcox and Mitchell (1977) carried out a small study that pinpointed one of the major issues of group acceptance or rejection. They were able to show that where a member of a group knew he or she was accepted by the group his or her self-esteem was thereby increased, and that the stress effect of the group task mattered little. Conversely, where a member knows that he or she is rejected by the group although retaining group membership – that is, he or she is not highly or even favourably regarded by his or her peers – then the stress response to the group task is enhanced. Both these responses are compounds of self-esteem and stress; in one case a double positive and in the other a double negative.

Yalom (1970) suggested that, when individual members of a group become aware that the group's judgement of them and their own judgement of themselves are discrepant, this creates dissonance.[1] One of the methods of reducing dissonance is to produce behaviour that will lessen the individual's anxiety, for dissonance generates a state of tension. Yalom thought that group members tended to move towards the acceptable patterns of group behaviour by imitation or assimilation.

So far we have suggested that knowledge of acceptance or rejection will be sufficient to set in train these consequences, but it must be recognized that a belief that rejection or acceptance has taken place will produce the same result. This brings into play the so-called 'as-if' syndrome, which means that observed behaviour is understandable only if the person is behaving 'as if' in response to some perception that is not an objective reality.

Rejection or the perception of rejection may of course be much more complete than was suggested in the Wilcox and Mitchell study, which, even though it comprised a complete statement by the group that the member was disposable, was a one-off occurrence in the life of the group. Repeated rejection over time pushes individual members further to the periphery of the group and, if leaving is a possibility, into physical absence. Sometimes rejection of this nature is accepted and tolerated by group members, who then remain to be constantly rebuffed and scorned, because this kind of behaviour is preferable to, and gives greater reward than, the known or available alternatives. This is often one of the major factors in the process of scape-goating.

Acceptance on the other hand provides the support that produces a tangible sense of security, warmth, and affection accompanied by increased self-esteem. The latter seems to be based upon the perception by the individual that he or she is being confirmed as a person and that others like and accept him or her as a worthwhile person and as an asset.

As long ago as 1955 Thomas Gordon was listing those factors that conveyed acceptance. Admittedly he found it easier to list all the behaviours that could convey rejection, but this is perhaps only going at the problem of acceptance by the back door. Gordon noted that some of the more important rejections constituted responses that indicated a desire to change others directly or indirectly, such as:

(1) Ordering, commanding, demanding, requiring, prohibit-ing.
(2) Obligating, persuading, warning, cautioning.
(3) Appealing, imploring, wishing, hoping.
(4) Advising, suggesting.
(5) Criticizing, condemning, devaluating, moralizing, judging.
(6) Giving information.
(7) Making interpretations.

He even suggested that approving, praising, rewarding, reassur-ing, agreeing, and supporting, all of which are positive responses, might actually convey rejection on the basis that the recipient might find them embarrassing. Which brings us to the crux of the matter.

Lists such as the above are amazing when read in cold blood. The only possible help they can give to groupworkers is to open up possibilities that they may not even have considered. But as a list they have no context. In the correct context, between the right kinds of personality, virtually any kind of response may be either wholly accepting or wholly rejecting. The form of address that is a virulent insult in one case may be used as indicative of long-standing and affectionate friendship in another. This is yet another example of the embedded nature of all human behaviour.

The thesis of acceptance/rejection is essential to understanding the power of groups to influence the behaviour of their members. I have covered this in some detail in previous books (Douglas 1976, 1979, 1983), and it must suffice here to reiterate mainly that as long as a group can be seen to accept an individual without charging him or her too high a cost for the privilege, he or she will usually remain a member. This idea produces some interesting spin-offs when the prospective member is unable to express any choice over the group he or she joins – a situation that faces a relatively large number of people in residential situations. The price in terms of satisfaction may be far higher than the individual wishes to pay in loss of freedom, say, but there are no alternatives.

Amongst the possible responses to the situation are readjustment of satisfactions by increasing those available elsewhere, rebellion, anger, apathy, and resignation. Some reassessment of the situation to reveal benefits previously unrevealed (a reduction-of-dissonance approach), or some form of withdrawal, is also possible. Withdrawal may be psychological or physical or both, but the kind of distance that can be created between members of a closed institution is fascinating and leads us to look at forms of isolation – a very peculiar relationship indeed, which is often dependent on the presence of others for its effectiveness.

ISOLATION

Social isolation is a difficult concept to define, and the reader may well wonder why it is included here.

> 'Nevertheless most theorists agree that alienation involves a dissatisfaction with one's social relationships as well as a feeling of loneliness . . . and that the majority of the antecedents and consequences of isolation are most profoundly related to one's interpersonal relationships.'
>
> (Berlin and Dies 1974: 462)

These authors are asserting that isolates are people who have problems with their interpersonal relationships, an obvious statement perhaps, but nevertheless one that can well stand reiteration. They go on to discover how group members with this characteristic inability to make satisfactory relationships fare within the group. Given that making relationships with others is one of the fundamental building blocks in the creation of a group, the end result may be interesting (see p. 3). However, there is a distinction to be made between isolation that is a choice of the isolate and isolation that is inflicted upon him or her, though as we shall see there may be common elements to both.

It is assumed here that fear of being faced with one's separateness, uniqueness, and inability to make direct communication with one's fellows is a fundamental aspect of human experience. Direct communication in this sense means communication without the need of the coding/transmitting/decoding process with the use of elaborate symbols capable of infinite misinterpretation like speech. Thus the associative and affiliative needs of human beings are very great, indeed essential, not least to affirm us as being alive and as giving indications of the kind of person we are. So the act of choosing to isolate oneself from others can be based at one end of the scale on such a sense of personal adequacy that others are not deemed necessary, or at the other on such a sense of apprehension, again real or unreal, of the hurt that can come from contact that the isolate state is preferred.

But, you may say, such people do not join groups! Such people are already members of groups like a family; the processes of education and work create groups; so this statement has to be amended to, 'Such people, once their attitude to isolation has been formed, do not join groups willingly.' Nevertheless they find themselves in group situations and maybe, as in some residential systems, in one from which there is little or no possibility of physical withdrawal. The element of choice has been largely removed. 'Isolation is merely a matter of isolating oneself, but total solitude is an oppressive thing and slowly wears down its lonely victim' (Bombard 1953: 144). Total solitude is not what people in group situations experience, but more what Raven and Rubin (1976) call being 'alone in the presence of others'.

Andrews described group members who chose to be isolates as 'persons who seldom express themselves, largely remain silent, but usually listen and follow well' (1972: 153), and commented that such isolates seemed to be essential in establishing a balance in a therapeutic group. This is logical, as they are representatives of one approach to social behaviour. Heap (1977) refers to such members as 'withdrawn' isolates to distinguish them from our second category, which he calls 'rejected' isolates.

Two comments are probably necessary before we look at this second form of isolate. Firstly, the 'withdrawer' can effect withdrawal only in the presence of others; he or she must be with other people in order to withhold contact from them. Withdrawal is therefore a social act precipitated by an awareness of others. It is possible in this form only in a social context. The response to this form of isolation is complicated by having to ascertain whether it stems from fear of hurt or from a perceived lack of need of others, or from both. In the first instance the behaviour can be changed only if the isolate experiences a reduction of the fear that holds him or her aloof. This needs experiential evidence not verbal affirmation to be effective. In the second case the isolate will tend to respond only to a realization that the group needs him or her and that he or she needs the group.

This analysis is far too simple, as isolate responses are often disguised by other behaviour like anger, violence, or silent obstruction; but it does express the fundamental principle of chosen isolation.

The second comment relates to the distinction that needs to be drawn between similar patterns of behaviour stemming from different sources. For instance, as we have seen, isolation is not total solitude, nor should it be confused with hugely different needs for privacy nor with a temporary need to be separate. The distinguishing factors are usually to be found in the frequency and time spent in an isolate state as compared with those spent in interaction and in the intensity of the commitment to that interaction.

An excellent example of the rejected isolate is offered by the phenomenon of the scapegoat. Once more there is a social group in which one or more members of the group are forced to the periphery of that group, not wholly out of it, and compelled to fill what is usually described as a major maintenance role for the whole group. There is little about this situation that occurs as a result of the conscious choice of the scapegoated individual, but there are usually some indications that he or she expected something of this nature to happen.

The literature of social psychology and of groupwork practice contains many references to this phenomenon (see, for instance, Berkowitz and Green 1965, Garland and Kolodny 1966, Mann 1967, Shulman 1967, and Feldman 1969), so only the cardinal issues will be presented here.

There are two basic ideas about the creation of scapegoats, namely: (1) that there is a 'scapegoat' persona and (2) that scapegoating is a phenomenon designed to keep the group in business. I think these ideas are manifestations of the same thing.

When a group begins to realize that something is wrong, when its goals are not being achieved or the wrangling is too intense, when apathy is breaking out, when there are great differences in the commitment or in the willingness to change, or when there is stagnation, then in order to preserve itself the group will start to look for possible reasons. As we said earlier (p. 13), the reasons that groups and organizations discover for their malfunctioning are often completely wrong because there is insufficient knowledge of the way groups are embedded in other groups and of the network nature of influence. A frequent gambit is to select one or more people as being responsible for the situation and to blame them for it — a convenient ploy, easily understood by all involved, and demonstrably popular as a reason for things going wrong throughout the whole of our society. Sometimes this explanation is the correct one. Far more frequently it is only partially correct, and more often still it is wrong. But it makes the accusers feel good. They have traced the fault, and it is not theirs. This is where the whole modern use of the term 'scapegoat' bears some relationship to its historical roots.[2]

The essence of this group manoeuvre is not to drive the faulty or blameworthy member out of the group, but to keep him or her in a position where they have little influence but are handy to be blamed for continuing problems: a very useful maintenance procedure.

How is the scapegoat selected? Rejection appears to be based upon several factors, which add up to the perception by other group members of difference and dislike. Let us take difference first.

Difference by itself in either appearance or behaviour is obviously not sufficient to create a homing device for scapegoating. When a group is going well, difference, within tolerable limits, seems in fact to be the source of new ideas, drive, inspiration, and movement. However, it is a well-documented fact (see listed sources on p. 145) that when scapegoating occurs the persons selected for this role are discriminated against for being 'different'. The difference chosen may be anything in the vast range of possible member characteristics – sex, age, race, belief, experience, etc. – but it is usually a relatively marked difference. Some would have us believe that there are personalities whose 'owners' are attention-seeking and who court this kind of isolation by their behaviour. It is true that for some of those with few social contacts a hurting relationship is preferable to no relationship at all. There are group members with sufficiently low self-esteem for whom this isolating and blaming process has all the aspects of a self-fulfilling prophecy and gratifies them in being correct in their estimate of their own worthlessness.

Mann's (1967) thesis about scapegoats lends itself to the idea that, because the group has reached a certain stage of development, those who cannot fully share in this movement become targets for hostility based on the perception by the others that they are (1) holding the group back and (2) threatening the unconsolidated and as yet fragile gains the group has just made. This is a special case of difference and is certainly accompanied by dislike and a certain amount of fear. In this case the isolate's behaviour might also be seen as provocative.

Maybe enough has been said to indicate what a complex relationship that of the isolate is. It can be seen to benefit the group by keeping it in existence; to be a probably ineffective way of dealing with group problems if they are not truly the fault of the person(s) blamed; to supply the attention needs of some group members and form a focus for some kinds of hostility that would otherwise be discharged into the group as a whole. One further point must be made; the isolate is always part of the group, even though the connection may be extraordinarily tenuous. If he or she leaves, then the group must find another to play the role or change to a different method of attempting to cope with problems.

In this vein, Garland and Kolodny (1966) list twelve techniques for the resolution of scapegoating, as follows: (1) squashing, (2) altering the composition of the group, (3) giving information to the group about scapegoating, (4) protecting the scapegoat(s), (5) diverting the group's attention, (6) reducing the level of interaction, (7) giving ego-support to the scapegoat so that he or she can change their method of dealing with hostility, (8) clarifying the situation for the group, (9) focusing on the scapegoat and his or her needs, (10) encouraging the group to take control of the scapegoating activity, (11) playing out the situation, and (12) removing the person(s) scapegoated. The last technique will give the group a chance to create new maintenance techniques to replace the lost scapegoating procedure.

FRIENDSHIP

The factors of interpersonal attraction are without doubt very important in the formation of friendships. But as most of the material relevant to friendship in groups is already covered in chapter 5 of *Groups: Understanding People Gathered Together* (Douglas 1983), it should suffice to indicate briefly here some new factors that have been put forward.

It has been assumed that if the factors supposedly generating friendship could be reduced, then friendship would dissolve for lack of sustenance. Shapiro (1977) discovered the following facts about friendships formed during a summer camp:

(1) When friends who were highly attracted to each other were separated on the grounds that proximity and contact are effective

maintainers of friendship, it was discovered that as often as not the intensity of the relationship was increased. The effect of separation was to increase the feeling of liking in order to balance the fact of separation.

(2) When friendships were formed between individuals where large dissimilarities existed, then keeping them together was more likely to dissolve the friendship. An increased level of contact and interaction served only to highlight the differences between them.

Shapiro went on to postulate that in professional helping relationships two factors might be important: (1) short-term professional relationships would minimize the possible discovery of essential differences between helper and helped; and (2) enduring relationships could create a situation in which essential differences became no longer of much importance in terms of the helping relationship.

There is also the factor of difference to consider. When friendships are based upon some basic similarity, but that similarity is itself different to the norms of the group, the friendship stands a good chance of enduring. This is not surprising in that the friendship is then a deviant sub-group, and each member of that sub-group is aware of his or her dependence upon the others within it for survival.

So although all the factors of interpersonal attraction operate in the formation of friendships, their maintenance and their dissolution are concerned with the context in which they exist and with the time over which they endure. Similarity may not be as important in this process as we have hitherto assumed, and as a result of this, complementarity and the increase of rewards take on greater significance. But ultimately, as with every other aspect of group life, it is impossible to understand friendship except in the context in which it is embedded.

GROUP-LIVING RELATIONSHIPS

Many hints have been given in the preceding material of the importance of relationships in a group-living situation. Interpersonal attraction cuts across all kinds of social division, as does friendship. It is interesting that until fairly recently much time and effort was devoted to discovering what brought about these relationships but very little to what dissolved them.

Personal relationships depend to a great extent upon choice, upon contact, upon similarity, upon reciprocity and friendship. In a residential setting choice is often restricted though not by such a great margin as many suppose. It is generally thought that choice is unrestricted in 'normal' situations, but a moment's thought reveals this for the gross error that it is. Most ordinary social situations offer extremely restricted choice, though they are somewhat less restrictive usually of the possibility of changing the situation than residential settings are. Many people in these 'ordinary' social situations are, or can be, extremely isolated, and this may not be from choice either.

It could be argued then that residential settings offer more contact amongst a limited population who all have very obvious similarities than many a situation outside. Add to this the factor that pushes people to make supportive relationships in order to survive in situations that contain a perceived element of threat – which will then bring about that acceptance of individuals who might have been rejected otherwise – and you have a fairly potent relationship-forming system. Indeed this can be seen to occur and in particular it tends to happen by affirming the two major sub-groups in an institution in their separate identities.

However, it does not always occur in this way. One of the major reasons may well be the non-voluntary nature of the residents' presence in the institution. An alternative set of relationships can exist in memory and in fantasy. Shapiro's (1977) interesting analysis of the separation of highly attracted friends demonstrated an increased intensity in the friendship in some cases. Thus the past may be much more real and acceptable than the present. There is a great deal of evidence that this particular technique was widely used amongst prisoners of war who made no 'real' contacts amongst their everyday companions, when they had any, but who had stimulating and supportive relationships in their minds with people of their choice from the past and even sometimes from an imagined future.

The factor of time is also important. When groups have been together long enough their members know what to expect; some of the fear of the unknown has been removed. But while time can provide knowledge that lends itself to security, it can also demonstrate differences not in evidence earlier. Depending on the nature of those differences and upon the context in which they emerge, they may add to the expectation and familiarity pattern – but they could also expose the relationship to have been founded on a basis that was not at all what it seemed at the time.

Time also demonstrates the difference between transient and more permanent relationships, as well as displaying the basis upon which they were formed. It also reveals the different rates at which the members of a group change or respond to pressure. Where change is an expected pattern of life, those group members who do not change in step with the group become exposed to all as being 'different'. If change is important, then those who drag their feet are likely to be put under pressure and even to be scapegoated.

Relationships within a group-living situation should be seen not as confined by the walls of the institution but as a nodal point, a focus, where the strands of influence, experience, and patterns of past behaviour of a collection of individuals meet and are held for a brief period of time. Then the experience of that situation is added to the previously existing system and it changes. Relationships within the setting, the setting within the organization, the organization in the society, and all the individuals in the context of their past and the immediate present form a complex matrix that we can never wholly understand, but we can at least be sensitive to its possible and probable influence.

NOTES

1 A full explanation of the thesis of 'cognitive dissonance', a term first used by Festinger (1957), occurs in Aronson 1980, chapter 4.
2 For those interested in the biblical version, see Leviticus chapter 16, verses 10–22.

7 The Environment

In the search to create a definition of 'a group', most ideas put forward have been essentially related to the disciplines of the researchers.

> 'Each discipline has assembled its own typology of groups in order to further understanding of interpersonal relationships within the parameters of a given field of study.'
>
> (Ellis, Werbel, and Fisher 1978: 415)

The result has been a state of chaos in which comparisons could hardly be made. One factor more than most that seemed to be cavalierly treated has been the environment in which groups exist; so much so that it was possible to have a discussion about a group as if it was a wholly discrete and independent entity. At best the influence flow between group and environment has been seen as one way, i.e. group on environment or the reverse, but seldom both together.

Ashby (1968) described a group as a 'self-organizing system'. Because organization involves choice, certain actions, patterns of behaviour, relationships between events that are selected in preference to others, the idea emerges that this promotes constraints. The next step was to see that constraints could come from two basic sources: either within the group so that it was self-limiting, or from outside it, i.e. externally governed.

Lazlo (1972) defined the group as a self-organizing system that consisted of a relationship, a balance between self-imposed constraints and those asserted from outside the group. The nature of this balance was felt to be essential to understanding how a group functioned and in particular the relationship between a group and the next larger system that contained it. Often enough this relationship has been described as 'tension' existing between the group and its containing system. I have come to call this process 'embedding' and the influence that crosses the boundary of the group in both directions 'seepage'.

Ellis, Werbel, and Fisher (1978) proposed that groups could be clearly and unequivocally defined in terms of their relationships with the containing system. For instance, they called those groups and groupings that reached out into their containing environment, giving out information like any task-oriented or decision-making group, 'extensive groups'. In all Ellis and colleagues defined six kinds of group based upon this particular relationship. Another typology of groups, to be sure, but this one has some direct implications for the residential setting in terms of the way in which groups are planned.

After all, one way of looking at a residential establishment is that it is a specifically created environment, created in such a way that its main functions are facilitated. For instance, when elaborate technology or rare skills are required in the treatment of some illnesses, it is infinitely more efficient and economical that these resources should be concentrated in one place, which can also provide accommodation for those who require to use them. The sheer numbers of those requiring a particular facility also dictate that they be gathered in one place so that the economies of size and concentration can be effective. In essence then a residential establishment is a defined environment in which the process of the institution can be facilitated.

Thus the environment of the establishment becomes a very important factor in the residential process, ranging all the way from the atmosphere or climate that it can generate through to the quality and nature of the resources provided within it. But because environments, buildings, access, location, space, resources, etc. tend to be accepted as given, little cognizance is given to the possible influence they can exert until it is made manifest or until the time comes when an environment is to be specifically planned to meet certain needs. When the latter situation arises it soon becomes apparent that the correlation between environmental factors and the effects they can produce on the humans who inhabit them is under-researched and consequently little understood.

There are many reasons for this. One of the foremost has been a basic assumption that, as long as the quality of the people involved was good, then their surroundings mattered little; and to a considerable extent this is often true. As an argument in favour of neglecting the physical environment, however, it is very poor, in that the use of the physical structures often continues far beyond any particular group's term of occupancy of them.

The problem of the charismatic leader is a case in point. Many examples exist of residential units being established where the driving force was the energy, foresight, ideals, and personality of one person or of a small group. The very enthusiasm and dedication of these people carries them, and those who work with them, through a whole barrage of obstacles; in order to achieve their aims they agree to work in environments – physical environments, that is – that would be wholly unacceptable to others in their field whose personal charisma is of a different order. The result is often a thriving community in which small miracles are performed and in which the poor quality of their environment is seen as a blessing rather than a curse.

But the major problem has already been stated and occurs when, for whatever reason, the community loses its charismatic leader or leaders, often because they are people for whom there is a total lack of challenge in a relatively smoothly running establishment and they feel the urge to start again somewhere else. The result is usually chaos. The structure of such establishments is clearly revealed at this break point to have been founded on a personal-relationship base, which while eminently effective is also extraordinarily fragile. It may have been sufficiently supportive for other influence systems hardly to matter at all. But they do matter with increased emphasis when the relationship structure no longer possesses its star attractions. The establishment, if it is to continue, has to create an enduring system, not an ephemeral one.

In simple terms a system founded on a relationship structure is too narrowly based and extremely susceptible to destructive change. This is not to say that charismatic leadership is useless, far from it, but it does need to be based in a structure that will survive the withdrawal of the leader(s) with minimum loss of efficiency. One of the elements in this broader base must be the environment.

The problem, already highlighted, of the lack of knowledge about the causal effects of the environment can be shown simply in the following illustration:

A large city authority decided to establish a mother-and-baby home. It bought a large country mansion and proceeded to take mothers from inner-city slum areas for training in the basic care of a family with a guarantee of a place to live back in the city when they were considered ready. Two factors were overlooked: firstly, that the country house presented an environment that was wholly alien to the mothers in terms of simple factors like distance to shops, lack of traffic, no familiar landmarks, lack of people, quietness, and the immense size of the rooms. It took weeks to get a working adjustment to this alien environment. Quite a few could not make it and left. Secondly, having adjusted to this kind of environment the prospect of a return to the limited space and poor amenities of the council's proferred accommodation caused some of the mothers to refuse to relinquish the standards to which they had become accustomed and they would not go.

It is well understood in Northern Ireland, for instance, that children from the two religious communities, when brought away from the sectarian environment of Belfast, can learn to live, work, and play, and trust each other. But the effect hardly ever survives a return to an environment where friendliness to the 'other side' is regarded as some kind of traitorous activity, against which sanctions are brought into play.

So the environment creates pressures that can either support a group or help to destroy it. The problem as it is presented here has to be given finite parameters because the seepage-of-influence effect could be expected to be infinitely extensible (see p. 18 on consequences). A reasonable cut-off point must be found where it becomes unrewarding to pursue the possible influence effects further. In large organizations with designed administrative structures the cut-off point has to be made on the basis that unpredictable intervention is a remote possibility – often not an easy decision to make. For instance, small units operate within large hospitals with minimal interference from the general management structure; but the possibility that something may make the small unit an item of concern and thus subject to the influence of the large organization is always present. Such an event has to be given an estimated 'probability-of-occurrence' rating and its effect must be allowed for, while the business of daily functioning and the more specific group-related pressures are given a much greater proportion of the available concern.

CONSTRAINTS

Constraint is defined in *The Concise Oxford Dictionary* as 'confinement', which means that limits are placed and boundaries set. In common usage being constrained tends to mean 'held in' or 'restricted', subject to compulsion to do less than one is capable of, so that an imprisoned person is held under 'constraint' or is 'constrained'. Thus there is a strong tendency to see constraints as undesirable. But while the limiting function of constraints is wholly acceptable, the negative connotation is not.

Groups have demonstrated countless times that if the boundaries of operation within which a group exists are understood then that group will tend to function much more effectively than another group similarly constituted but operating in ignorance of its situational constraints. Thus the first point to make about constraints is the need to be aware of their existence, because ignorance of them does not reduce their effect but only makes much greater the possibility that misunderstanding of the nature of their effects will arise.

The second point is that constraints have several very positive functions in terms of definition, support, etc. For instance, safety (p. 81) tends to reside in knowing where boundaries exist. The testing behaviour of children over a period of time creates for them the limits of the space in which they have discovered they can act with freedom, which equates with their knowing what to expect. Hence the idea of the value of the consistent response, which ensures that energy has not got to be continuously devoted to checking and re-checking because each time the results are different. This is a most effective method of generating uncertainty.

The third point is that in a general sense anything can operate as a constraint. Once more the interlinked nature of all factors becomes clear, and once again we have to operate a cut-off point in taking constraints into our working consideration. Some constraints are patently obvious, e.g. the quality and potential of group members, the resources available, the skill and knowledge of leaders, the environment in which the group is held. But within these large general areas are smaller ones to which attention is sometimes but not often given, largely because the extent of such constraints is hard to ascertain.

A consideration of these three points should illuminate the nature of constraints and also lead us directly into a consideration of the thesis underlying them: the principle of embedding.

As I have said before, time is one of the major constraints, and one that is clearly understood in some aspects and wholly misunderstood or ignored in others. It can serve to illustrate all three points.

Let us take a group that meets regularly once a month. Its members attend regularly and put in a large amount of energy because they are groupworkers and are committed to this monthly meeting as a form of support and as a system of sharing experience and information. Over a long period of time, several years in fact, the main feeling about the group is that it is barely rewarding, yet each session on its own seems to have had quite a lot to offer. What is wrong? The fact is that the expectations of the group members of what can be achieved in terms of development for a group that is held monthly are quite absurd. So much time, so much experience, so much obliterating material, so much hard work with other people, takes place in the time between groups that with the best will in the world each group is almost a new experience. The sense that each group has something to offer is created by the fact that each one is two hours long, long enough for a bunch of groupworkers to work hard enough to generate sufficient rehabilitation of relationships to be able to use the resources of the group for about the last half an hour.

The problem arises because the constraint of time, in this case too much time, was ignored in the design and setting up of the group, but it takes its inevitable toll. What is gained has to be worked for much harder than if the group were fortnightly or weekly. Then it would not need to be so long because the time-lapse constraint would not have made the re-creation of the members' relationships to each other a necessary and time-consuming prologue to working together.

An alternative would of course be to re-design the group to take into consideration this drastic effect of the lapse of time. Given the fact that the group in question has inconsistent attendance, such a re-design becomes essential. The time lapse itself would have a much less damaging effect if the membership of each session was identical. Any re-design in this situation would involve the creation of a structure that would alleviate the necessary re-establishment of working relationships.

The structure of choice in this case would be an accepted series of rules of procedure that would allow members to slot into a known and accepted role with a relatively set relationship to all the other roles. The programme for the group would be worked out in advance, and the leadership would be directive, maintaining the input and interaction within the defined parameters. What would be lost if this were done would be a certain freedom to respond to the immediate situation; the level of emotional involvement would be maintained within a pre-set tolerance. What would be gained would be an increased satisfaction in that the group would be performing a useful function and that constraints and negative effects of unavoidable time lapse and irregular attendance would have been reduced. Any group member would know that at any particular group session where he or she could slot into the process, even though he or she may have missed several sessions, the whole of the two-hour period could then be devoted to the purpose for which the group was established. The time constraint would then become a positive rather than a negative factor.

Indeed this group demonstrates equally well the way time as a constraint is linked into all the other group processes – in this case to energy input, achievement, satisfaction, cohesion, etc.

In essence what we need to look at now is the way in which all systems form part of larger systems and contain smaller systems within themselves to infinity. Without some understanding of the embedded nature of systems it is possible to see constraints only as the isolate manifestations of such embedding, and thus any attempt to design a group system that takes such isolated phenomena into account can at best be only partially successful. Like icebergs the major part of any system or systems is hidden, and its presence, though unsuspected, will influence all parts of the situation with which it has contact.

THE NATURE OF EMBEDDING

Goroff (1971) noted what he called 'an intersystemic frame of reference' as one of the three basic components of social group-work. He described it as the relationship between the individuals and the group and their environing social and cultural systems; a complex of systemic linkages with a variety of groups, which, along with the relationships among individuals, sub-groups, and the group as a whole, and the dynamics of the group itself, determine an influential intersystemic frame of reference for the group, whether cognizance of it is taken or not.

There seems to be a strong correlation between the intensity of personal involvement in a particular group and the inability to see the influence on that group of factors existing outside it. Thus consequences arising as a result of external factors are often unfortunately ascribed to influences operating within the group. One example should suffice to illustrate this point.

In 1983 the staff of a residential intermediate treatment unit had come to the conclusion that the reason they were being noticeably unsuccessful with their residents was that their group-work skills were not of a sufficiently high standard to cope with the problems they had to face. Given the training background of the staff and the lack of really credible groupwork courses available, this was not an illogical assumption. In the event it was only partially right, but the groupwork skill they lacked was not that of running groups in their unit; it was the skill of being able to see how those groups and the unit as a whole fitted into an overall programme of dealing with their residents and how this overall strategy laid down constraints that mitigated against the performance of successful groupwork as the groupworkers understood it.

The major constraint in this case was that the length of stay of a resident was governed by factors that related to the needs of the legal system and broke the period of residence by periods of absence in different locations. Given the disturbed state of the youngsters involved in the scheme, the time required to create trust, to remove suspicion, to begin constructive work in bringing about change, was just not available. What most residents produced was a kind of public conformity with the system as it presented to them. This is a survival technique and allows only the commitment of that degree of involvement which will ensure that the individual will 'get by' and no more (see p. 97).

Inevitably such a low level of commitment does not augur at all well for a group programme based upon achieving at least some minimal change. Resistance to change takes place in this situation not so much in a direct challenge to the system, which would indicate an investment of a fairly high order, but more likely by a form of restraint that looks uncommonly like apathy at a surface level. This restraint is not evenly distributed over all the activities of such a unit because perceptions about what activities pose a threat and which do not promote different responses.

This kind of problem often arises when people design systems, residential or otherwise, to meet apparent and assessed need in the absence of adequate understanding of how constraining and constrained the design will be. That the people who are brought in to operate it also have an inadequate knowledge of one of the main skills of their profession only compounds the problem. For, given a knowledge of the way groups are embedded in larger groups throughout any system, the response should not be, 'We will try to make this work', but 'In this form this system will not achieve the ends that are sought.' Of course this is a difficult statement to make; a job is a job, and optimists are always sanguine that their presence in a system will serve to make it work. But what follows tends to be a desperate searching for reasons for the lack of success, a lot of bad feeling, and maybe even rejection of any form of groupwork as a wholly unpromising approach.

Sometimes the constraints that embedding can create are neither as obvious nor as straightforward as the example just quoted. Nor are they wholly or even often negative in effect. Constraints are often supportive, creating boundaries and defining the possible. The problem is not the constraints themselves; it is rather that we do not recognize them for what they are and get ourselves into all sorts of tangles by ascribing their effects to wholly inappropriate causes.

A second factor is that groups set up without due consideration of the effect that the containing system will have are almost certain to produce problems. For example, Cohen, Robinson, and Edwards (1969), experimenting with communicating levels for task-performing sub-groups embedded in larger and more complex organizations, found that when members of the sub-group oriented themselves to the containing system, a greater degree of subversion of the communication system within the smaller group occurred. In effect the authors were suggesting that there is little possibility of understanding the behaviour of any small group in isolation from the larger system in which it is embedded. In this respect it is necessary to consider that large groups are the containing system for the smaller groups existing within them. Thus any large institution will have many smaller groups within its confines, some of which will be permanent and some transient, but the tension that exists at the boundaries of these groups large and small will provide a major part of the energy for their continued existence.

The idea of the 'embedded' nature of groups needs to be understood as part of the interrelatedness of all group dynamics. Commonly in a group situation it is accepted that change even of a very minor nature in any part of the group produces consequences for all the others parts, some obvious and predictable, others never usually even considered. But this analysis of what occurs in a group can also be made up and down the scale; up into large-scale organizations and down into sub-groups and individuals, none of whose behaviour is understandable in its own right but only as part of the context in which they exist. It becomes interesting to speculate on the quality of the assessments we make about the behaviours of individuals and groups when so many of the interlocking current and past networks of influence having some effect on the perceived behaviour are wholly unknown or ignored.

As this is a major theme of this book it is worth pursuing it further. Indeed every aspect of group life, right up to how new-comers to the profession might be taught, is fundamentally concerned with this theme.

As groups are embedded in larger groups and contain within themselves sub-groups, so every individual member of all these systems is embedded in and sustained by a complex set of strands of experience and his or her interpretation of them. In some ways each individual is a focal point into which feed all the experiences of his or her past, current known and unknown influences, inter-pretation of all this (how he or she has stored it in his or her data bank), and current perception of the situation in which he or she is. Certain of these strands are, or will become, more important than others and therefore are more dominant in directing current behaviour. They may be more dominant because they are seen as more important or they may be so because they are habitual and well used, almost unassailable by more recent influences.

Thus no human being can ever be more than partially under-stood, and that only in an extremely unbalanced way, except in the context in which he or she exists. As that context itself is unlikely to be totally understood – (1) because of its com-plexity, (2) because there is no available record of most of it, and (3) because the interpretation of it is idiosyncratic – we must accept partial, unbalanced understanding as all that is possible. However, this is no reason to accept that there is no value in making the attempt to understand at all. If all that happens as a result of trying is that we become more aware of how what we know probably fits into the much larger pattern that must exist but at which we can only guess, then our understanding has been enhanced.

A recurring factor in groupwork literature is the 'hidden agenda'. This phenomenon is described as containing factors that influence the behaviour of group members but are not known to other group members. Specifically hidden agenda has been taken to be a programme that the individual has for him-or herself and that the group as a whole does not know about. Often there is an implication that this agenda has been established by previous unsatisfying group situations and may therefore be buried deep in the individual's mind, a motivating force unknown to the individual.

Groupwork literature tends to create the impression that the 'hidden agenda' and the 'unfinished business' syndromes, while occurring with reasonable frequency, are not ubiquitous. I would strongly disagree. They are the commonest of common phenomena, but it is only when their effects become noticeable in a given situation that they are accorded recognition. They are part of the contextual pattern of the individual, part of the resources that he or she brings to the group. The cyberneticists show us that systems can be self-governing, that they can be supported and maintained, kept within set limits by feedback on the consequences of their performance. The ultimate effect of embedding is that a complex system of feedback of effects and consequences is created from myriad sources.

We cannot remove people from every source of previous feedback because memory is available under most circumstances. But there is clear evidence that, when removal does occur – through illness, change of location, artificial separation, physical handicap occurring where none previously existed, and so on – major stress can be created. If new feedback loops can be established then all will be well, but where this is not possible then deterioration becomes inevitable.

RESIDENTIAL ENVIRONMENTS

The basis for many of the ideas expressed here has come originally from systems theory, but more particularly from the work of Gregory Bateson adopted into social work in much diluted and somewhat distorted form in the work of Pincus and Minahan (1973). Hints about the interlocking systems of which any particular group is part have also been around in group-dynamics literature for some time (see the start of this chapter).

Among the reasons why many practitioners accept almost without question the nature of interlocking systems and are wholly aware that they can be described as a complex series of feedback loops, but yet cannot come to terms with the idea in practice, is that even to start to describe such a system and to track an event through it involves an enormous strain upon the language used. More importantly, it entails the possibility of maintaining a multi-dimensional picture of the systems involved, which are in a state of flux. It is natural in these circumstances that a cut-off point occurs; given the obvious difficulties of tracking in such a system, that cut-off point is often very close to the behaviour or situation under scrutiny.

In order to attempt to diminish this problem the twin concepts of 'embedding' and 'seepage' have been stated. Crude though they are as tools of analysis, they at least point in the direction of increased awareness of the complexity of the factors combining to produce a situation.

In residential environments the problem becomes acute. The very sense that the situation is defined by the confinement of residents tends to limit perception of the major networks to two: 'inside' and 'outside'. I have heard residential workers say that their institution was free and easy with minimal rules until faced with behaviour that they found intolerable. Almost immediately there appears a complex web of rules, where previously none existed, of acceptable and non-acceptable behaviour, and often there is little argument about them. Where did they come from? The truth is that they were there all the time, subtly influencing behaviour, but never made explicit. Often they appear to have been a process of accretion over a period of time so that what might be called a 'culture' develops. Culture in this context is a structure of traditional practices the unspecific nature of which is usually highlighted by challenge.

It is not possible to challenge something that does not exist, so the existence of challenge or the perception of challenging behaviour must rest on the presumption of some accepted order, however nebulous or unspecified.

It is very easy to restrict our consideration of environment to the material structure in which a residential system operates. But environment is in reality the total system in which residents exist and this includes other residents and staff. It must also include the atmosphere, the structure, the traditions, and the history of the institution and to some extent the expectations of those living within it.

There is little doubt that the way residents regard the system in which they live can have an enormous effect upon their behaviour. This effect is tangibly present even in groups whose occupation of a particular institution or part of an institution is for only a couple of hours or so once a week. The same group can perform very differently in an environment that they see as hostile or relating to some experience in their lives associated with feelings of hostility, to how they act in one where they feel at ease and comfortable with a strong sense that the environment is friendly.

The intangibles of environment, the ethos, and the atmosphere are often very important in the influence they have. Some people are sensitive to atmosphere, others less so, but it is certain that when that climate is related to a change from familiar to unfamiliar surroundings most people's sensitivity is increased.

A group of young mothers formed a club to further their leisure and educational activities. The only property that was available to them in which they could hold their meetings was part of the local health centre; to be more precise, one of the clinics. Having accepted the venue, they quickly found that the atmosphere of the clinic, its connection with part of their lives significantly different from their current use of it, its smell, its posters, etc. all helped to militate against their enjoyment. When another venue was made available without such clinical connotations some weeks later it was accepted with alacrity, and the club expanded into a much more comfortable and enjoyable existence. This is a simple example of the effect of atmosphere based upon a short period of time spent in a particular building. The effects of atmosphere in those institutions that are total living institutions for their residents must therefore have the potential of being vastly greater.

8 Some Central Issues in Group Living

In *Groups* (Douglas 1983) I compiled an incomplete list of what residential institutions could do in order to give a flavour of the wide range of residential possibilities. Payne gave a shorter list of the aims of residential care in which a knowledge of group behaviour and skills in groupwork were deemed to be important:

'1. in developing and managing the "natural resources" of group living;

2. in identifying, managing and mitigating the many tensions and stresses encountered in daily living;

3. in facilitating the integration of the newcomer to the residential setting and, correspondingly, in helping him to prepare for departure from the setting;

4. in providing opportunities for personal development and life enrichment;

5. in helping residents find solutions to the interpersonal and other life problems that have often been the cause of their admission to care;

6. in helping residential staff to exercise constructive and creative leadership in particular through a continuous process of appraisal and review of the events and happenings of residential life.'

(1978: 60)

Like all groups, residential groups display a plethora of tasks and goals. Some of these are compatible, others are not; some are open and acknowledged, others are secret; and some are unknown or at least unrecognized by those who pursue them. Groupwork literature bulges with references to these facts, and as they are readily available to all who need them it is not my purpose to repeat the general concepts of group tasks and goals here. More particularly there are certain residential group tasks and goals that because of being more specific to residential situations deserve illumination from groupwork literature. For example, conflict within a residential establishment is something most people seek to avoid. Many reasons may be offered for this aversion, ranging from expediency to the perception that excess conflict, or conflict of a very violent nature, diverts energy that could be used more constructively in another form and thus inhibits and diminishes therapeutic endeavour.

For some residential establishments conflict is a significant problem. Most of their residents adopt conflict as at least a major behavioural and social pattern. But apart from the traditional procedures handed down by word of mouth, what training do residential workers get in conflict management? Drugs, an equally violent response, time-out, and coercion are all part of the traditional response patterns. Some learning about violence and aggression may have occurred on training courses, but because the techniques of conflict resolution and management have been formulated in a significantly different area of human existence they have seldom been either known about or imported into the residential scene.

Wilson and Ryland said: 'Conflicts and their solutions become the central core of any activity of any group operating in any medium of human interest' (quoted by Cowger 1979: 310). Once more we are faced with the realization that practical knowledge founded in techniques has been, and is, available over a much wider range of human activities than is ever used, but it tends to get forgotten or mislaid.

Information about the way people behave in groups has of course been accumulating at a fantastic rate over the last forty years, not just in one sphere of activity but in many, ranging from riot-control methods, methods of organization, hijacking, and other terrorist activities, through football crowds to families, religious sects, and various therapies. Unfortunately people operating in one sphere seldom seek information from another; new ideas are regarded with suspicion and in any case require an effort of will to master, while traditional practices have the blessing of time and familiarity.

CONTAINMENT AND CONTROL

Perhaps the most obvious fact about residential situations is that in a very direct sense they 'contain' their residents. Groups of any kind could be said to do likewise, but the duration of containment varies considerably. The factor of 'containing' has some interesting material in the group literature ranging all the way from the psychological containment of reference groups to the encapsulation of some treatment groups, which can produce insights about the enclosing situation of group living but is seldom directly referred to as containment.

I therefore think it is essential to start from some brief discussion about containment, because the restrictive and constrictive nature of this concept is often regarded with abhorrence by those who prize freedom. Some form of containment, both physical and psychological, is however a necessary ingredient of effective living. The major inducer of disorientation amongst us occurs when the stable patterns of our existence are changed or removed. This is much more confusing when the change is quick and also when it is brought about by others.

As we have already said, we tend to be held in a network of the familiar – people, places, objects, routines, relationships, which, while taken for granted because they grew relatively inconspicuously, are nevertheless the factors enabling us to make sense of our existence good or bad. We are, almost without knowing it, constrained and contained by the known and familiar environment. What does create problems is when, beyond the ability we have to intervene, these containing factors are removed or changed, and others, often not of our choice, are substituted.

We need, then, to consider what evidence we have that would inform the way in which such dramatic changes of containing factors are made or that would help in ameliorating the consequences. Containment must surely be looked at in two separate ways: imposed and voluntary.

When an individual is placed within a group or group-living situation at the instigation of some other person or organization, whether or not he or she ultimately agrees with the placement but where he or she did not initiate the request for the change, then the placement must be deemed to be imposed, brought about by some form of coercion. This is not to say that efforts to increase the amount of information and/or its quality about the proposed change, which will allow for an informed choice rather than one based in ignorance, should necessarily be regarded as coercion or even persuasion. However, much experience goes to show that the way in which an individual is constrained to enter a group situation is largely instrumental in conditioning his or her response to it for a considerable period of time. Thus where an individual chooses on the basis of an assessment of his or her situation to enter a group or a group-living situation, then his or her entry is voluntary, and the set of expectations so engendered will be significantly different even if the situation should ultimately prove unacceptable. Much the same result is achievable if the client involved is wholly unaware that any form of pressure is being applied, but to work on the assumption that this is so brings into focus a large ethical problem.

These two aspects equate with external and internal direction. Some writers, notably Reisman (1950), have suggested that we are either dominantly 'self-directed' or 'other-directed'; therefore responses to suggestion might well be personality features. But there is a general 'containment' by the networks of society and social patterns in which we live that is so universal and ubiquitous that until crisis occurs we are seldom aware of them. So when we move, the containing systems change with a consequent loss of safety and certainty. Thus the element of control in a group situation is directly related to the quality and the acceptance of the containing element.

Hartford, quoting Thibaut and Kelley (1954), says they 'found that a group could not induce control over its members greater than the strength of the members' motives to belong' (1972: 252). She went on to define group control as the influence individuals and sub-groups have upon each other and upon the group, brought about by 'the significance that they come to have for each other'. This highlights once more the essential factor of time; enough has to elapse for the members of a group to discover what significance the group and the members of that group has for them and whether it forms an acceptable substitute for lost support systems. Of course time is not the sole factor of importance, as the quality of the relationships and the nature of the impact of the group can either increase or decrease the length of time required to make this discovery.

Hartford (1972) proposes that group control can be seen to have four sources, namely: structural, interpersonal, coercive, and cultural. We can discuss group control under these four headings.

(1) Structural control

The structure of groups has been dealt with in Chapter 3 and included the structure of influence. Thus it suffices to say here that the organization of power, or at least the perception of its distribution, is instrumental in defining control.

> 'Through designated functions or collective action within the group, the leadership provides structural control through regulating individual impulses, co-ordinating the power and interests of the members, creating a collective authority and exerting pressures to keep members in line with the general will of the group.'
>
> (Hartford 1972: 264)

This kind of structural control is more obvious where the structure of power is clear-cut, e.g. in hierarchical systems where different levels have defined limits of power. But even where the power structure is not an organizational creation it can exist by virtue of the perceived qualities of the group members – for example, charisma, physical or mental stature, the possession of qualities deemed by the group to be of great worth, affectionate ties or other bonding factors, and so on. Power may reside purely in the ability to be innovative or to initiate action, but it is operative in all cases only so long as it is believed to exist or be useful to those over whom it is exercised.

Even legitimate power becomes authority if it is not recognized as power by those who exist under it, and it will then need the production of fear, the exercise of sanctions, and the availability of force to maintain it.

Thus behaviour within a group is finely tuned to the members' perceptions of the power existing within it or that can influence it. Control depends to a large extent upon this perception, and different perceptions of its existence and quality within a group or between groups leads to some very interesting conflict situations, especially where power is confused with authority and is not backed by adequate force.

(2) Interpersonal control

As the subheading signifies, this control system is based upon personal relationships existing within the group and thus ultimately upon individual perceptions of other individuals' qualities. They may be based on attraction and thus positive, or negative based upon repulsion, but their overall effect is to condition behaviour that enhances acceptance and diminishes rejection by 'significant' (to the member, that is) others.

The influence of attractive members often spreads despite any intention on their part by what Redl (1942) called 'behavioural contagion', a process of emulation. 'Reflected glory' or the concept of value 'rubbing off' also expresses the same idea. Control is effected as always by limiting the repertoire of behaviours to those that are acceptable; in this case the limiting factor is internally applied – 'This is the way I should behave.'

There is some evidence that emulation is strong when people are unsure of how to behave acceptably and take as their models others who appear to be confident of their role and to enjoy high status within the group. Where rules and norms are not clear, this form of imitation buys time to acquire the necessary experience that will allow an informed assessment to be made of what is required.

(3) Coercive control

Although Hartford uses this term to indicate the kind of pressure that the group can bring to bear upon its members which stems from the cohesive nature of the group, it would probably be better described as pressure towards conformity. This kind of pressure is dependent not solely upon the cohesive nature of the group but upon the perception by the individual of what he or she stands to gain by continuing to be a member. Thus this kind of control depends upon a fine perception of the balance of rewards and satisfactions perceived to exist in or out of the group situation, as we have seen earlier (p. 97).

Without doubt the greater the cohesion of a group the greater the pressure that can be exerted, because cohesiveness is dependent upon attraction to the group, which occurs only if high levels of satisfaction from being a member of it appear to be available.

> 'If a group develops a high level of cohesion, then the individual member will be caught up in pressure from the group to behave in accordance with group expectations if its norms of functioning are conducive to health, growth, action, and problem-solving.'

(Hartford 1972: 269)

There have been many examples in recent years when group pressures to conform accompanied by apparently very high rewards of membership have led what were originally ordinary people to commit most incredible acts; e.g. the Manson killings, whole religious groups committing suicide, or even extraordinary feats of endurance and sacrifice. This kind of control is certainly one of the most powerful influences in human existence.

(4) Group cultural control

'Group culture' is used here by Hartford in the sense of the normative structure of the group; that is, the patterns of acceptable behaviour it has developed (see p. 64). Golembiewski (1962) suggested that the control of behaviour exerted by the norms of the group was the strongest of all. Once again we are faced with the idea that if a group begins to have great meaning for an individual it can demand and get conformity behaviour of a very high order. 'Great meaning' in this context can be literally translated as fulfilling, better than any other known or available alternatives, one or more of the individual's more important needs.

Moreover if this level of need fulfilment is indeed high (see p. 98 on public conformity and private acceptance), then the behavioural changes brought about by the group persist in the individual's behaviour outside of it. In effect the changes are not transient and expedient but willing and much more permanent. The values of the group have been internalized to a great extent.

It is interesting to watch individuals come into a group and behave according to the accepted patterns of social behaviour of their particular part of society, overlaid by what could be called the more general patterns of the society as a whole. After a period of time the individual members begin to realize that some of these patterns are not only not useful in the pursuance of the group's activities but actually inhibiting. From this realization begin attempts to establish different rules that enhance the group's task performance, and a new group culture begins to emerge. When a group designs its own norms like this, the commitment of the members to follow the rules is very great, largely because, unlike with most rule-following, they feel they have a good element of control over what concerns them greatly; they have value and they have power.

Cultural control, then, is based upon the following facts:

(1) The need of members to be accepted by the group.
(2) The involvement of members in the creation of the group norms.
(3) The need to achieve status and position in the group.
(4) The fear of being seen as different.

Two other factors need to be considered: firstly, that many people are not aware of the values and norms by which they operate in everyday life. In fact they may well be confused about such matters. A group with clear standards, values, and norms can resolve this confusion and bring about an element of clarity, of certainty. The satisfaction that this can produce for some people is considerable; doubt is removed, there is the fellowship of others who are clearly following the same pattern, and isolation is dispelled. Not all people need such clarity, but at times of crisis even those who are normally content to live in a state of psychological 'free-fall' feel the need of the comfort of sameness.

Secondly, we must give some thought to the aspect of dilution. Most of us belong to many groups and derive what we can from multiple membership. This implies that the pressures which can be exerted by any one of the groups may only be relatively small unless we are singularly devoted to it, because there are probably several available substitutes that can supply our needs should one of the current ones fail by making our costs too high. But what about those individuals whose group memberships are few, in the extreme case perhaps only one, and who have no such substitutes? What are the problems of those who are restricted to membership of a group or groups over which they have little or no control and that, by force of circumstances, they are forbidden to leave?

In one case the devotion to the one group that exists may be desperate and unlimited because the prospect of non-membership is unbearable. In the other the element of constraint may be seen as preventing membership of much more desirable groups. Thus the power of the group over the first individual may be almost unlimited depending on the degree of his or her fear of the unknown (in most cases the pressure has to be appalling before death becomes a viable alternative). In the second case the power of the group depends on the individual's perception of a future escape from it and can range all the way from the group being presented with a high level of public conformity to a complete denial of any influence at all.

Perhaps the major point at issue here for all those involved in group living is that of the absolutely essential need of beginning to know and understand the perceptions of those who come into the residential scene. Most of the information available currently for residential staff does not contain this kind of data. As always, the starting point of working with people is the recognition of what is involved rather than a bland assumption of knowledge that may well result in not only hurt but conflict, which we must now consider.

CONFLICT RESOLUTION AND MANAGEMENT

'Conflicts in group process are the result of incompatible needs, goals, or values of group members and are often brought about by competition for leadership, time or the attention of the worker.'

(Cowger 1979: 309)

In my work with groups of people who are employed in residential or other group situations, a problem of groupworking that surfaces with inevitable regularity is conflict within the group. It takes many forms, e.g. the disruptive member or sub-group, the group against other groups, the group against its leader or other individual. Although other groupwork skills may be adequate, few workers seem to have received much instruction on the possible causes of such conflict and even less on its management. This section will concentrate on conflict resolution and management in groups, bearing in mind that conflict within a residential setting is often seen as being more intense than elsewhere, especially when the ability to leave a conflict may be restricted by the containing nature of the institution.

The whole idea of mediation is of fundamental importance, not just in small groups or even in large-group organization like residential settings, but in local, national, and international politics and in huge industrial concerns. The major problems of conflict have received a great deal of attention, but little has been devoted to attempts to apply what has been learned from resolving and managing large conflicts to such behavioural patterns in smaller units of organization. What has been attempted often indicates a predisposition to operate along the lines of conciliation and mediation, based upon particular concepts of the way in which human beings behave, without a clear assessment of what value conflict may have for those involved in it. In fact it is possible that such a value, whatever it is, may not even be directly related to the conflict issue at all, so that resolution of the conflict by management of those issues is never a possibility.

As industrial and political conflict has shown in this situation, mediation tends to reward the more aggressive and intransigent of those involved as the mediators seek concessions from the more amenable of the conflictors. Thus the whole purpose of mediation is frustrated as the aggressive party can only gain by continuing to be intransigent. Combined with the fact that conflict is sometimes created in order to divert attention from other problems and is thus defensive, and further that it may spring from some ideological commitment, the problem of analysis is complex. In groupwork terms it is one of the clearest examples of working to hidden agendas with all the consequences of assuming that similar behaviour in a given situation springs from similar causes. In small groups the possibility of resolution and management rests largely upon the exposure of these causes. In political and industrial spheres this kind of exposure of roots is neither easy nor often possible, because exposure is seen as weakness, or the ideological causes take the form of an almost religious faith which is held to represent a form of unchallengeable truth and is therefore in no way negotiable.

Cowger in his paper on conflict takes as his starting point that 'explicit practice principles are lacking for dealing with conflict' (1979: 309). He goes on to suggest that conflict in groups is natural and may have great value for the members; he ultimately outlines practice principles for conflict management. Frey (1979) includes in her paper definitions of conflict, its causes, stages of development, management and resolution, and the techniques involved. These two papers, which are essentially digests of some of the available knowledge about conflict, plus my own experience form the bases for the material offered in this section.

Personal conflict may be defined as a tendency to perform two or more incompatible responses at the same time, resulting in stress. The idea of incompatibility is central to all forms of conflict; whether it be open physical struggle or silent manipulative hostility, there is always a clash of ideas, wills, aims, direction, desires, etc.[1] Because of this sense of opposition, people generally regard conflict as bad; internal conflict generates tension, anxiety, and uneasiness; external conflict generates anger, frustration, fear, and hostility.

Conflict in groups may have any of three major focal points:

(1) Personal conflict – individual group members in a state of tension.[2]
(2) Intra-group conflict – members of one group in conflict with one another.
(3) Inter-group conflict – one group in conflict with another group.

These separate focal points are not mutually exclusive, and the last two are complicated by the definition of the word 'group'. Thus (2) may be seen by some observers as conflict between sub-groups in one overall group, but by members of the group concerned as a clear case of (3) – that is, as separate and distinct groups in conflict. The definition will depend upon the perception of difference.

Frey (1979) uses a slightly different categorization in which she includes as the object of conflict the environment. Thus she postulates an 'impersonal' conflict between the individual and material objects, resources, space, etc. familiar to us all. Frey lists five prime causes of conflict:

(1) Differences in information.
(2) Differences in interests, desires, goals, or values.
(3) Scarcity of resources, e.g. money, time, space, position.
(4) Exercise of power and status.
(5) Organizational structure – impeding requirements.

Terhune (1970) lists seven personality factors that predispose a person to either co-operation or conflict:

(1) People of aggressive or rigid nature tend to elicit conflict.
(2) Conflict is more likely when participants are defensive and when withdrawal is impossible.
(3) Among people who are mistrustful, exploitation and retaliation can occur.

(4) Co-operativeness is likely among those who are passive and dependent.

(5) When co-operation is the best resolution, those who are flexible and success-oriented will be most likely to comply.

(6) Co-operation is likely among those who are generally trusting and egalitarian.

(7) Factors of insecurity and/or resistance to change, rivalry, and some forms of competition that include putting others down can be important.

Two general factors are to be added to this list:

(8) Poor communication.

(9) Differing perceptual sets.

This is a fairly long list but it clearly demonstrates the functions of the perception of difference, the experience of frustration and of personality factors. All these factors can work in at least two directions, however, so that we must look at the value of conflict.

Frey (1979) says conflict may be one of two types: (1) Functional (constructive); that is, the conflict exposes issues that have been impeding progress and results in an improved quality of problem-solving. It also increases emotional involvement, creativity, cohesiveness, and the establishment of group norms. It may also produce an element of clarity about the group's aims. (2) Dysfunctional (destructive); that is, the conflict tends to escalate, diverts energy, weakens morale, obstructs co-operative action, increases differences, and can cause psychological trauma.

Northen (1969) suggests that functional and dysfunctional states of conflict can exist together. Yalom maintained that conflict brings 'drama, excitement, change and development to human life' (quoted by Cowger 1979: 310). Cowger writes that 'groups that confront and deal with conflict are more productive' (1979: 310) according to evidence from small-group research. My own view is that conflict is such an essential and ubiquitous form of human social behaviour that groups must therefore reflect at least an equal proportion of conflict and, given that some groups enhance the causative factors of conflict, an even greater proportion. It must also be true that if the understanding available to those groups tending to generate conflict is at a better level than is found in society in general, then such conflict could be more functional than dysfunctional.

Frey (1979) shows that conflict develops through stages of latency when the potential for conflict exists: through the awareness by members that misunderstandings have developed and through the stage when 'large constellations' of feelings become engaged (e.g. bitterness, feeling unloved, frustration, depression, anger, hurt, loneliness, guilt, sullenness, vengefulness, fearfulness, being uncomfortable), to the manifestation of open conflict and the release of tension through aggressive behaviour or through hidden means. This is all followed by the aftermath, the consequences of such a release, and whether it was successful in bringing about not just a release of tension but also a resolution of the causes, or whether it generated more causes, whether it released tension or not.

Frey draws a distinction between conflict management, which she defines as 'the reduction of tension in the conflict in order to enable the person to pursue his or her goal' (1979: 125), and conflict resolution, which aims to reduce the conflict and to dispel it to the satisfaction of those engaged, by attempting to understand its causes.

Palomares (1975) listed seventeen conflict-management strategies, which could be used separately or in combination, as follows:

(1) Negotiating – talking about one's position in the conflict and what can be done about it.
(2) Compromise – both sides to give up something.
(3) Taking turns – each side being given an unfettered opportunity to express itself.
(4) Active listening – each side being requested to listen to what the other is saying and to indicate what has been heard by repeating it.
(5) Threat-free explanation – one side attempts to communicate its position without threatening the other.

  (6) Apologizing – one side can say it is sorry without having to say it is wrong.

  (7) Soliciting intervention – the groups involved can consult other sources of expertise or prestige.

  (8) Postponement – the protagonists agree to defer discussion to a more appropriate time.

  (9) Distraction – someone or something else is made the focus of attention, thus diverting and/or defusing the situation.

(10) Abandoning – the protagonists leave the conflict situation in order to minimize harm when it cannot be dealt with.

(11) Exaggeration – a blown-up version of the conflict is discussed (or role-played) so that protagonists can see clearly what its components are.

(12) Humour – if it does not ridicule or insult, this may help reduce tension and ease resolution.

(13) Chance – resolution based upon an arbitrary event like tossing a coin can help the protagonists save face.

(14) Sharing – the use of equality, each side treating and being treated alike in sharing feelings ideas, etc.

The Palomares list is quoted in Frey's paper, and she adds at this point that 'the remaining conflict strategies are not pro-social and have numerous negative consequences' (1979: 128). They are, therefore, not recommended.

(15) Violence – verbal or physical abuse; 'get it over with'; not an effective strategy in most cases.

(16) Flight – retreat physically or psychologically; at worst this creates a deterioration of self-esteem.

(17) Tattling – the involvement of others to handle the conflict.

These strategies were originally produced for children; but, as Frey says, most adults, having no training in conflict resolution, are like children in this matter.

  Cowger (1979) produces the following management principles for the groupworker:

(1) Conflict should be confronted and dealt with, not avoided, to contain any diversion of energy away from the group task.

(2) Intervention should be structured in a manner that enables group interaction to avoid win/lose situations.
(3) Process should be clarified and interpreted.
(4) A relationship with the whole group should be maintained by the worker.
(5) Standards or ground rules should be set.

Cowger means that conflict should not be allowed to become a festering hidden agenda; nor should it be cut off before its beneficial effects have been maximized (what Cowger calls the 'optimal tension level') – a very difficult choice. Any intervention based upon a clear win/lose situation may only serve to generate sufficient resentment to ensure energy for the next conflict. The idea that what is being done is understood and that apparent bias should not enter into it is a long-standing principle of groupwork.

Factors that are important in the intervention in conflict management as listed by Cowger are: the self-awareness of the members; their ability to control their behaviour; the quality of their communication skills; their ability to withstand stress; and above all timing. Shulman (1967) discusses what he calls 'stepping down a strong signal'; that is, reducing the strength of a communication so that it can be understood by those to whom it is directed – e.g. reducing shouting, angry tone of voice, or intensity of facial expression – as a technique that will allow retreat without loss of face.

When a resolution of a given conflict is proposed it is well to bear in mind certain factors that are obstacles to success. What has been called 'conflict blindness' is a good example. None of us are new to conflicts even if they are only quarrels, and over the years we develop habits and styles of conflict participation. Situations contain cues to which we respond by triggering set patterns of behaviour, and differences in a situation tend to be ignored because of our hypersensitivity to our own particular conflict cues. We are, in effect, blind to what else exists in the situation. Then the impulsiveness of our choice implies that the patterns we will activate as a response are nearly always the same. Many people talk of being trapped in quarrels, knowing that they are setting in motion a long and hurtful process but apparently unable to respond differently. The cause may be that what could be different is almost wholly unknown to them.

Thus approaches to conflict resolution must start with recognition of difference, which may be possible only when some level of trust adequate to hold such an exchange has been created. Threat can be reduced by reasserting the personal strengths of those involved, the good things; and by instituting a process common in effective groupwork of checking the accuracy of the messages. 'This is what I heard you say. Is this what you meant?'

Another kind of checking-out concerns the assumptions involved on both sides. Often they are widely disparate, based on a lack of information or on material that is incorrect. A valuable question to ask is, 'What are people trying to achieve?' The answer may well lie outside what appears to be the centre of the current conflict. When alternatives are sought in a conflict it is often the case that readily acceptable ones either have been ignored or are not known about; but when alternatives are looked at it is very necessary that the consequences of any choice should be considered. Whatever approach is used, then, part of the resolution is contractual planning to put the choice into operation and equally a contractual review to monitor progress and perhaps to modify obligations as the situation changes.

Perhaps the greatest difficulty in conflict resolution is the almost universal belief that it is not possible. This can usually be countered by producing evidence of successful resolutions, detailed to include causes, feelings, styles of conflict, and the stages of resolution. Once the sense of the inevitability of damage in conflict is dispelled, and it is established that habituated perceptions and response patterns can be modified, the feeling of being trapped in a familiar pattern can be relieved, and effective work towards conflict resolution can take place.

It must be said that there are people who enjoy conflict and promote it way beyond what most of us would find acceptable. Such people cannot respond to the approaches detailed here unless other social patterns of equal or greater levels of satisfaction can be offered as substitutes. As such people are already experiencing satisfaction from socially dysfunctional behaviour patterns, finding adequate substitutes that are both acceptable to the person concerned and pro-social is a very difficult procedure.

THE EFFECTS OF FEEDBACK

'Many authors contend that feedback is one of the most important processes which occur in group interventions. Yet a surprisingly small amount of knowledge exists regarding the most effective manner of delivery of feedback. The major problem arises from the fact that neither the delivery nor the reception of feedback is solely an objective transfer of information, but both arouse strong emotions.'

(Jacobs and Spradlin 1974: 408)[3]

It may seem peculiar that 'feedback', which is so often solely understood as a technique used in some forms of personal growth groups, should concern us here. But Wiener (1948), who coined the term, defined it as 'the alteration of a system's input via its own output, by means of a closed feedback loop' (quoted by Jacobs and Spradlin 1974: 409). Translated from physics, this means a system that regulates itself by monitoring its production; in other words it learns by means of a self-reviewing process.

If we can assume that group-living situations are seldom regarded as perfect by those within them, then it must be equally true that methods of improvement are being continually sought. It has been stated many times that all human beings tend to operate as if their perceptions of a situation were accurate until (and not always then) evidence to the contrary is seen to exist. Thus the members of any group make assumptions about each other, about the group's performance, about the leaders, etc., all of which will form the basis for their subsequent actions within that group and all of which may show a wide range of diversity and difference. For instance, Lundgren found that early in a group's life the group members' attitudes corresponded closely with their perceptions of the trainer's attitudes to the group and their perceptions were accurate; but the trainer's perceptions of the members' attitudes to them were almost invariably wrong. Later in the group there was a change towards a closer matching of attitudes, but Lundgren estimated that trainers 'consistently and strongly underestimate the favourability of participants' attitudes towards themselves.' (1975: 387).

Because members' attitudes to leaders are so favourable it is to be expected that inexperienced and untrained leaders will get an overrated opinion of themselves as effective leaders. This suggests that there is a clear need for feedback to be associated with other methods of performance-rating. This also needs to be accompanied by a much clearer understanding of what is involved in the process of feedback.

Thus the efficient functioning of a group depends to a high degree upon two facts: firstly, on a recognition of the existence of a wide range of diverse, probably conflicting, and consequently damaging assumptions; and secondly, on a method or methods of making this obvious and probably of forming the basis for techniques of reducing the efficiency loss for the group. The former can be dealt with by the use of information, but both aspects of the latter may be dealt with by the appropriate use of feedback.

In groups feedback is the verbalization or otherwise, the conveying of perceptions about behaviour, outcomes, feelings, etc., that allows the pooling of impressions which would otherwise have remained hidden but influential. The sincerity and honesty with which such feedback is given have greatly concerned researchers, as has the difficulty that most people find in getting close to their own perceptions (or being able to verbalize them to others if they can). Social behaviour and traditional practice do not prepare us adequately if at all for such direct response behaviour.

This poses a great problem. The delivery of feedback may be modified by many factors relating to acceptable social behaviour, and its reception may include a host of responses ranging from totally ignoring it to being devastated by it. Discussion of these problems can be split into the following two areas:

(1) What kinds of situation permit feedback to take place?
(2) What methods of delivery facilitate open reception?

Most group research shows that some feedback about behaviours and feelings occurs spontaneously between group members who work together for a long enough period of time. Thus there is evidence that the nature of feedback changes over time, so that attitudes about the group and its members tend to draw closer together and to become more accurate. But the major factor influencing this development is a complex process usually referred to as trust. In essence trust is based upon the ability to predict, which in turn is based upon the experience of a number of situations that have demonstrated acceptable outcomes in greater proportion than unacceptable ones.

This needs qualifying because the ability to predict may serve only to develop enormous defences if the experiences upon which it is based have been almost wholly unacceptable to the individual. Prediction may, under these circumstances, produce an element of safety, knowing what to expect, but will never develop trust, which requires that the predictions are of a likelihood that situations will generate satisfaction as well as security. Thus although time is a prime element, allowing memories of sequences of events to be stored, the quality and value of those sequences for the individual are equally important.

Where prior experience of group conditions has been deficient in this latter aspect, then either more time or a better quality of experience or both are required to overcome it. Thus where feedback as a monitoring system is essential, it is necessary for group leaders to recognize that it is a skill that needs to be learned and that there are certain necessary conditions for its nurture and development.

Positive feedback is seen as more acceptable than negative and as being more accurate, particularly if it is of a personal nature. So a starting point for the group is non-personal feedback that is positive, graduating from behaviour to feelings. The latter are very difficult to deal with, not least because we are not well versed in the expression of our feelings; awkwardness is inhibiting and is often overcome only when the feelings to be expressed are powerful, often only when powerfully negative, e.g. anger.

Gauron and Rawlings (1975) suggested guidelines for the giving and receiving of feedback for new members of therapy groups, as follows.

Giving: talk about the behaviour you can see; make it specific; make it relevant; give it as soon as possible; give it directly, don't hint or filter; give the other person a chance to explain; give it caringly; an attack is not feedback; don't nag or harass unless asked; don't be judgemental; avoid referring to causes of behaviour – you don't know; tell how you feel; be direct; avoid sarcasm and condescension; share the positives too; don't advise – just react.

Receiving: ask for it; receive openly; don't make excuses; acknowledge its value; don't be just blank; express appreciation of the care that motivated the giving of feedback; discuss it; view it as part of an ongoing exploration; indicate what you intend to do with it; don't become defensive; avoid getting angry, seeking revenge, ignoring the feedback and the person who gave it; don't look for hidden motives or meanings; seek clarification; think about it and try to build on it.

These guidelines relate of course to personal feedback, but they contain the essentials of what makes feedback acceptable and the basics of delivery. What can develop is a group wherein similar behaviour patterns are more likely to stem from similar motivations than is usual, and the group can begin to develop a common base for its operations, cutting down the need to spend time and energy on dealing with emotional and behavioural conflict.

Different residential settings will produce different needs for feedback, but much behaviour by members of such group-living situations that is attributed to personality factors may well stem from misunderstandings of that situation. These might arise from perceptions of it or of parts of it that are significantly at odds with either the general design and purpose of the situation or major parts of its everyday procedure. Explanation, to be effective, must have meaning; that is, it must relate to the information already possessed by the receiver in a roughly similar way to how it related to the information possessed by the person offering the explanation. This can be one of the basic strengths of groups comprised wholly of people who have gone through a similar major life experience and one of the weaknesses, in terms of separation, of institutions containing a managing sub-group that has not had the same major experiences as the managed.

As most of the current research on feedback in groups is gathered in two main papers[4] and thus readily accessible, the main thrust of this section has been to put forward the idea of feedback as a review procedure. If a climate favourable to review can be created then a method is available to measure what is going on, not in terms of some abstract criteria, but in the perceptions of those involved. The answer to the question, 'Does it work?' is brought out in terms that are relevant to the needs of those who are part of the system rather than in terms that satisfy the statistician or the economist. But because our society generates people for whom the idea of sharing, (and in particular sharing perceptions of others, unless it is to be critical) is an ideal which is not to be observed, the whole process of feedback has to be taught, practised, and learned in an appropriately supportive milieu.

THE ASSIMILATION OF NEWCOMERS AND THE DEPARTURE OF ESTABLISHED MEMBERS

Some of the literature on groups deals with the phenomenon of the closed group – that is, a group that starts with a given population of members, which remains unchanged throughout the life of the group. As far as possible no one leaves the group during its lifetime and no new member is added. This kind of group offers the researcher an element of stability about the group, to which all events occurring within it probably bear an observable relationship. But for most people working with groups it is a phenomenon that at worst never occurs at all and at best is only partially true. For a given period of time, long or short, a group may have a static membership; so all the factors relating to a closed group begin to function, with the possible exception of the expectation of continuing membership.

For most groupworkers, the groups with which they work either have an erratic membership attendance pattern or are a processing system into which members come and from which they leave after variable or set periods of time. Nearly all residential situations fall into this second category, and thus most of the information derived from closed group systems is usually only of passing interest except for those institutions where the period of stay is very long for a majority of the residents. One of the big problems facing such through-put systems is consequently the process of induction and assimilation of new members. Patterns of accepting new members range all the way from formal, even ritual, procedures through informal methods to an almost straight rejection of the idea that anything special is required or beneficial about such a process at all.

For instance, Paradise (1968) thought that the entrance of a new member to an established group may generate anxiety and hostility detrimental to the group process. He suggested that at any of the five stages of group development – namely: (1) preaffiliation approach avoidance, (2) power and control, (3) intimacy, (4) differentiation, and (5) separation – the impact of the group upon the new member would be significantly different, and the integration process would need to be differently designed. This view indicates not only that some care is required in the introduction of new members but that it has to be varied to suit the stage to which the group can be seen to have developed.

The research and literature on small groups offer some ideas that may be of value in this situation.[5]

One other factor needs mention here. The problem of admitting newcomers to an existing group has a reversed problem in the fact that established groups have members who leave, and the group continues to exist after their departure. This must be considered in any review of the assimilation of newcomers, because it is as good an example of a process that, though extremely ordinary, is often forgotten, particularly in terms of its consequences, and that is the exclusive nature of choice. Simply, by choosing to be somewhere, to do something, to behave in a particular fashion, we are eliminating for that time the ability to be somewhere else, to do something else, or to behave differently; we thus set in train a particular set of consequences. The inclusive nature of groups is often stressed because it can and does engender a tremendous sense of being wanted and of belonging for those who are members. But it must be remembered that the other side of positive inclusion is the exclusion it demonstrates for non-members.

For example, in a residential unit for the physically handicapped all residents were accepted into the general programme of training and rehabilitation. However, the management trained some of the staff as groupworkers, and groups were held for residents with special problems. Although the facility was available for all, its basic purpose created the necessity for selection. Selection is apparent to all in a residential situation and in this case it created a strong sense of élitism and of being 'special'. Even if the method of selection was partially to blame, the obvious fact of inclusion/exclusion, so clear in residential communities, was probably a more important factor. This factor is clearly described in McCullough's (1963) article, 'Groupwork in Probation', which was concerned with selecting and working with a group in a probation hostel.

Crandall (1978: 331) collected together research from different disciplines to present the difficulties involved in integrating newcomers into established groups and the ways in which these difficulties might be dealt with. The problems he described may be listed as follows:

(1) Stress may be created for both the newcomers and the organization.
(2) Newcomers tend to exhibit more conformity and do more routine and less important work than established members.
(3) Some newcomers can exhibit depression and have serious problems relating socially and culturally to the new milieu.
(4) Newcomers are often inhibited in their actions.
(5) Newcomers may be subjected to dislike and hostility.
(6) Newcomers may experience role ambiguity and lack of assimilation.

(Item (1) comes from organizational research; item (2) from studies of judges; item (3) from work on immigrants; (4) and (5) from studies of children; and (6) from students.)

Newcomb wrote:

> 'The arrival of an outsider changes the situation both for him and for the group, setting in motion reactions to the change and processes of mutual adjustment which may or may not be satisfactory in their outcome. In any concrete case these processes are probably complex, being subject to the inter-action of a number of variables, such as age of the group, its function in the larger society, its relation to other groups, its organisation, how members in the initial group feel about one another, what the new person seems like, or is like, why he comes, etc.'

(1957: 500)

This may seem an enormous number of probable problems for the simple admission of a person or persons to a group. But we must remember that a group is a system, and an additional member creates the possibility of a large number of new relation-ships plus the disturbance of others in prior existence; it provides the possibility of new and different resources. Above all else, the newcomer, whether ultimately or immediately of benefit to the group, has not shared the experiences of the group prior to his or her entry into it. However similar his or her experience has been, it has been undergone with different people to the newly joined group members. The newcomer and they have not gone through the process of being able to predict each other's behaviour from increasing familiarity, which is a significantly different factor from being *au fait* with the routine behaviour patterns of the group, i.e. its norms, rules, pro-cedures, etc.

All the problems listed above tend to be related to this aspect of personal unfamiliarity. They are responded to in different ways according to the personality of the newcomer, ranging from fear, through caution, to aggressive brashness, take-over bids, or attempted independent existence.

Crandall (1978) listed in his paper what researchers had found to be probable techniques for dealing with these problems:

(1) Preparation by giving information to both group and prospective member

It is often difficult to know what kind or extent of information is of most use. We frequently assume that overall structural information is most valuable because we fear not to cover all aspects of a fairly complex situation. Experience shows, however, that such information means nothing because the newcomer has no context into which it will fit and therefore finds it confusing; or the newcomer already has information of his or her own from sources he or she tends to trust more readily and therefore will tend to discount 'official' information as at least biased. The group also has specific needs, in terms of information, which may be better understood.

(2) Presenting appropriate models of behaviour

This implies demonstration, rehearsing, role-playing the process of admission to familiarize those involved with the procedure. It cannot cope with the personal relationship factor, but it tends to reduce the awkwardness that is an added inhibiting factor.

(3) Training in anxiety management[6]

Most writers and researchers are clear that the introduction of newcomers to the group is an anxiety-producing situation. Therefore some understanding of the effects of anxiety and the development of techniques for handling it and reducing the element of threat should be beneficial. The extra problem here may be the lack of knowledge of threat-reduction techniques.

(4) Accurate information about the setting

This is specifically designed for the newcomer and includes: (a) the details of the setting both positive and negative; (b) the existence in the larger group of sub-groups or individuals with similar backgrounds, experience, or potential friendliness; (c) the possibility of satisfaction; (d) the use of sponsors for newcomers taken from the group.

(5) Introducing more than one newcomer at a time

This gives each new member at least one other person in a somewhat similar situation and the opportunity of sharing the process of assimilation.

(6) The management of impression formation

There is good evidence that the first impression of strangers governs quite a large part of an ongoing relationship. In the assimilation of newcomers, the group has to cope with unfamiliarity; and, as we know, the perception of difference can be fundamental in precipitating dislike. Crandall suggests that:

> 'If people were more aware of the importance of first impressions, they could be helped to express themselves better in new groups, and groups could be encouraged to avoid bias against others based on first impressions.'

(1978: 334)

Other factors that may affect how a newcomer is assimilated are:

(1) What habits the group has developed about admissions.
(2) How much the group needs new members.
(3) Whether the group is familiar with membership change.
(4) What the apparent value for the group is of the potential member.
(5) Whether the group has any choice in the selection of members.

As a rule, procedures that effectively facilitate the assimilation of newcomers are associated with a reduction in the drop-out rate at a later stage. Thus care at the stage of induction may well pay large dividends for the group in terms of stability of membership.

Some groupwork literature is now devoted to the process of terminating a group, once largely ignored. But it tends to cover the termination of the whole group rather more than the termination of one person's membership of a group that continues to exist. These are wholly different phenomena, but very few writers about groupwork seem to have devoted any space to the group member who leaves the ongoing group. Garvin refers to one member leaving as 'a modified termination process' (1981: 218), indicating that he believes it to be a special version of the general termination of a group. He suggests that individual leaving requires that the following should occur:

(1) Reinforcement of what the member has learned in the group.
(2) Work on the feelings about leaving.
(3) Transfer of the learning to new situations.
(4) Movement towards new resources.

Garvin also discusses the value or benefit to those who remain in the group when a member leaves and the leaving is well handled:

(1) It confirms them as people who are valued.
(2) It demonstrates that departures are not glossed over or ignored.
(3) It offers an opportunity to express their feelings of loss.
(4) It provides a rehearsal for subsequent departures.

Leaving a group is more difficult 'when the members and/or the worker view the group as unsuccessful in achieving its major objectives'. Garvin stresses that even when the group is unsuccessful it should still be evaluated, so that when the reasons for failure are discovered learning can take place about what to avoid in future group commitments. This latter procedure is essential in the process of beginning to understand and can usually be effectively followed only if some form of recording of the group's progress has been made.

Departure from a group is a reversal of the processes that brought about successful assimilation, with the exception that the duration of the experience of being a member has been added. Too often people leave groups because their time to leave has arrived, and little effort is made to consolidate the good that has accrued during the period of membership (see Chapter 9). This is wasteful and often hurtful; new learning requires that supports be established for it, which can be maintained in the face of pressures, usually familiar and possessing great validity for the individual, to revert to previous forms of behaviour.

It must also be stated unequivocally that newcomers and leavers in a contained situation, whatever sub-group within it they belong to, whether managers or managed, create ripples within the overall group. No doubt some are more productive of effect than others, but all add to or diminish the relationship structure, the available resources, and the organizational structure, at least at the level of contact.

According to the position an individual holds within an organization, the effect of others coming and going will be greater or lesser, but most of all the perception of the effect will be different. For instance, to staff the departure of one of their number concerns the loss of a colleague varying in kind according to the value that each places upon him or her; for residents such a departure may be the apparent betrayal of trust, the loss of the sole stable point of their existence, or alternatively a possible blessed relief, all dependent on each resident's assessment of his or her need of that staff member.

Comings and goings are now much a part of everyday life and little regarded in a society that not only is highly mobile but has progressively abandoned its rites of passage – ceremonies that facilitated the transition from one state to another. Consequently, when even the few markers still remaining are apparently obliterated, when we find ourselves in 'artificial' organizations, it is not surprising that people feel bewildered and confused. There is a great need to create points of familiarity, which can act as anchors to give people in transit some stable reference points; otherwise, as old people can demonstrate, the diminution and depletion of familiar landmarks results in confusion and the replacement of social contact and reality by withdrawal and fantasy.

DISCUSSION

This chapter has presented material from groupwork knowledge about some major issues of group living. There are just one or two points that need to be added and a couple more that require re-emphasizing.

Millham *et al.* (1981) listed the following as familiar sanctions in residential setting for children:

Inappropriate controls

(1) Corporal punishment; the reasons given for its inappropriateness were:
   (a) many successful institutions did not need it;
   (b) those using it extensively were ineffective in other ways;
   (c) it is usually applied to those least likely to be affected by it.

(2) Transfer:
   (a) it disrupts continuity of care;
   (b) it generates a problem child out of an initially irritating one;
   (c) those using it are usually the least successful.

(3) Group punishments:
   (a) are ineffective in checking a general drift to indiscipline;
   (b) they tend to encourage scapegoating;
   (c) group pressure can be extremely coercive.

(4) Limiting access to the outside world:
   (a) encourages isolation and increases dependence;
   (b) diminishes family relationships.

(5) Public disapproval:
   (a) creates an inability to distinguish trivia from serious violations of group norms;
   (b) may develop isolating styles – engendering a 'we/them' polarity.

(6) Secure rooms:
   (a) have a bad effect upon other children.

(7) Drugs:
   (a) indicate a failure to establish relationships.

Appropriate controls

All the remarks in this section were concerned with what Millham *et al.* called 'the *ethos* of the institution that controls by fashioning a system of mutually held expectations, values and norms of conduct, which exercise restraint on members' (1981: 48).

It is interesting that all through Millham *et al.*'s (1981) research paper there is stress on the fact that the excessive use of sanctions occurs when the power of the community to control its own behaviour has either never been created or been dissipated as a consequence of actions that have destroyed the true power base. What is then substituted, as was said earlier, is the application of authority backed by force.

It is wholly inappropriate to apply the techniques of conflict management and resolution to a situation that has the essentials of conflict generation built into it. Attitudes cannot ultimately be disguised in the close confines of the group, especially in group living; disparate responses become obvious, and the whole issue of game-playing takes on a paramount aspect.

All the group ideas developed in this chapter are underwritten by an attitude towards working with human beings suggesting that all forms of behaviour are ultimately rational and understandable when they are seen in the context of the individuals who produce them. Thus one way of approaching work with human beings is to attempt to discover what the world looks like from their point of view, which admittedly is difficult and daunting. But if groupwork demonstrates anything it is that such an approach actually works. The major limitations to its being adopted are that it involves time, patience, a great deal of hard work, a considerable amount of knowledge, and some sophisticated practice skills. It is, however, an approach that can also be defeated relatively easily by a lack of agreement to work with it by some people in any one institution – a delicate situation when placed against a chronic inability to forecast consequences and/or a tough-minded egocentrism that brooks no compromise.

Any residential institution is a system – or, more appropriately, a series of interlocking systems, all of which need a supply of energy to be kept operational. Very frequently what energy is available is directed towards maintaining the system in existence, and virtually none is directed to what the system is in business to do. The problem is that the members of the system are aware that they are expending an amount of energy, but are often wholly unaware what proportion of it is productively used. Feedback in some form is perhaps the only process by which an estimate of the effectiveness of a system can be made. The efficacy of any social system can be judged only on its ability to adapt, based on feedback on the consequences of its performance.

NOTES

1 Still one of the most comprehensive and rewarding syntheses of intergroup hostility and conflict, though compiled nearly forty years ago, is Williams 1947.

2 This kind of personal conflict is usefully described in Festinger's thesis of 'cognitive dissonance', a clear exposition of which, with comments, occurs in Aronson 1980, chapter 3: 99–157.

3 The paper by Alfred Jacobs quoted here, 'The Use of Feedback in Groups', which occurs in Jacobs and Spradlin 1974: 408–48, is by far the best and most detailed analysis of the subject.

4 The second is Reddy and Lippert 1980, which appears in Smith 1980, chapter 3: 56–84.

5 For detailed consideration of the different natures of open and closed groups, see Douglas 1979, chapter 4: 88–90. Admission to and departure from residential care are the subject of other books in the present Residential Social Work series; see Brearley *et al.* 1980 and 1982, both of which should be consulted for factors relevant to entering and leaving a group not exclusively focused on the group dynamics of these events.

6 See, for instance, Woods 1972: 201–11, in which this method of overcoming the initial resistance and ambivalence of parents is noted.

9 The Consolidation of Experience

All the way through this text the necessity of seeing and of understanding the 'embedded' nature of all groups has been stressed. When discussing this in terms of created groups Moore argued that there is

> 'the system network external to but transacting with, the group. There are two types of systems in this network: the other social systems of each group member (e.g. family, employment, community), and the systems to which the group as a whole belongs (e.g., agency, interagency network, society).'
> (1978: 133)

There are of course more networks involved than Moore stated, but the number is almost irrelevant. What is important is what Moore describes as 'the member's re-entry to those external networks' – that is, what happens to the adaptation, the integration, and the learning created by the internal networks of a residential system when the members of that system have to return to the outside world, to the external system. Moore was writing about group members leaving their groups and in all cases she would be referring to members whose existence in this particular group would be only a small part of their everyday life. The external system would still be around them for much the greater part of their life, and yet there is sufficient evidence from the literature to indicate that to leave the group even under these circumstances poses problems of re-entry.

A residential system can occupy a much greater share of a person's existence than a therapeutic group. In fact some residential systems reduce the external system to virtually nothing, a fleeting contact, a memory; the two systems can be reduced to one: the 'total institution' of Goffman's (1968) phrase. Thus the problem posed by re-entry, if re-entry is at all possible, must be of infinitely greater complexity.

Earlier in this book, mention was made of the ideas of public conformity and private acceptance (see pp. 97 and 175) and of motivation to change. We need to look now at the evidence available about the retention of change when the circumstances in which it was engendered are removed. We also need to consider how much the support system of the group and its milieu can maintain change and what may be the effects of change to a large system (society) where that support system does not exist and where there may be powerful countervailing forces.

The evidence about the maintenance of change given no further support other than what is generally available after leaving a group is not very heartening. Guinan, Foulds, and Wright made a six-month follow-up study of a marathon group and found 'that all participants of the marathon group perceived or felt it effected changes in them that appeared to have lasted' (1973: 180). Change is a very difficult thing to measure. The subjective and fairly coy nature of this statement tell us only that people felt changed, and there are many reasons why people should say this, very few of which may be related to true experience of change.

P. B. Smith says: 'A good deal of measurable change does occur after groups, but there is a substantial fade-out of these effects in subsequent months' (1980: 46). Smith was writing about the outcome of sensitivity training; lest it should be felt that such training groups are not relevant to other kinds of group, let it be said that this is not true. Sensitivity training groups are specifically geared to effecting change, many of the techniques used in them have become commonly used in all forms of groups, and in any case the group processes manipulated are the same for all groups.

Katz and Schwebel looked at the ability of members of training groups to retain and use their learning in the work situation. They found that:

'the subjects began to identify resources in the organisation and in others which they had not previously tapped and began

seeing others in the organisation as being more open. Con-
comitantly, they also began using their own resources more
efficiently, and more fully channelled their skills into dealing
with work problems.'

(1976: 282–83)

The general thrust of Katz and Schwebel's explanation of these
changes was that attending the group had given the participants
time to think through work problems in a systematic way devoid
of the anxiety of having to do their reviewing in the work situation. It does not seem to be in doubt that groups can and do
effect change in their members; what is much more problematic
is whether these changes last and what factors support their
continued existence. Of course if the changes were either
cosmetic or survival-oriented then, as we have noted several
times already, when the situation that brought them into being
changes or ceases to exist or to have relevance, the changes,
being expediency measures, will also disappear – unless they
have been continued for such a long period of time that they
have become an habitual pattern of behaving and exist in their
own right as routines no longer consciously monitored.

In order to explore these and related problems we need first to
look at what is known about the fact of the transfer of learning.
We are reasonably sure that groups can effect change; how can
it be transferred?

TRANSFER OF LEARNING

A universal problem of all change situations relates to the
transfer of learning. By this is meant that if learning – that is,
change – can be induced in a specifically created situation like a
residential institution that nurtures change, how effectively can
this new behaviour be transferred to other situations which are
not only non-nurturing but often distinctly antagonistic to the
changes engendered?

'Learning that is laboratory bounded is of interest, but it can
be dangerous because the individual could leave, feeling that

the only world that is a good one is the one in the laboratory. Such a conclusion would hardly lead to motivation to become more interpersonally effective in the "real world".'

(Argyris 1967: 162)

It does not require much imagination to see that this comment is applicable not only to laboratory groups, about which it was written, but also to all groups that have some vested interest in bringing about change in their members within a normative system designed to do just that.

Miller argued that strong cohesion in a group that facilitates interaction 'may create a sense of the group's uniqueness which limits the members' abilities to transfer training to outside situations' (1976: 222). Miller maintains that most groups seek to promote a bonding between members, a cohesion, because this ensures the continued existence of the group, promotes satisfactions for its members, and generates a supportive system in which members can feel able to acquire new behaviours. He cites the fact that members of groups often believe 'their group experience was something new and important in their lives'.

Oshry and Harrison (quoted by Miller 1976: 223) considered that, although members of a two-week group demonstrated a great increase in their understanding of interpersonal behaviour and resources, they showed no increase in their awareness of how this enhanced sensitivity and understanding could be used to solve the problems of their everyday world. It is one thing to be enabled to see one's world in a different way in a system particularly designed to do just this, and something else entirely to translate that perception into different behaviour. Miller suggests that a cohesive group produces a strong emotional response in its participants, which may be a new experience for most of them; this would lead to a strong commitment to the group, which in turn would tend to divert commitment away from the group's purpose, i.e. some form of change, to the group itself. Such a shift might in some senses be beneficial but it tends to create a dependence upon the group.

Kanter (quoted by Miller 1976: 224–27) analysed the factors that generated and maintained commitment in communes:

Renunciation   literally to break relationships with those outside the community. This was often achieved by isolating the community, a factor often present in a great many residential situations.

Sharing.   The communes made long-term contracts to share all things, but even the lesser acts of sharing – of work, accommodation, leisure, food – are expressions of communality. Meetings of the entire community were also a powerful pressure towards the engendering of commitment. After all, one of the main differences between members and non-members is the amount of experience they have gone through together.

Rituals.   Many group exercises, performances, common practices are affirmative of commitment to the group.

Mortification.   By this Kanter meant the trust that allows people to expose their weaknesses, problems, uncertainties, and failings with others; in other words, to perform acts of self-exposure. This, incidentally, is often the procedure by which a newcomer becomes an accepted member of the group. Confession, scrutiny in public of private lives, and mutual criticism are all seen today as acceptable forms of precipitating personal growth, but they are equally seen as investment in the group and thus part of the mechanics of the development of commitment to it.

Transcendence.   Kanter did not mean anything mystical in using this term, merely that members often develop a sense of the existence of great power and meaning in the group, which is far greater than themselves.

Charismatic leadership.   Sometimes this is a reality, sometimes it is a myth, but leaders are invested with power by members because this ensures that they themselves will be secure in the care of such leaders. Whether real or no, charismatic leadership often generates the factor of transcendence mentioned above.

Institutionalized awe. Kanter referred here to the growth of a group ideology that contains a theory and explanation of behaviour and some clear promise of future advantage for members. Decision-making in small matters is the concern of all, but major decisions are kept from the ordinary members and shrouded in some mystery. This process intensifies the sense of the powerful protecting group – see above.

The effect of generating intense commitment to the group is of course to create a 'them and us' situation in relation to the world outside the group, which makes transfer to that outside situation a hazardous procedure.

Amir (1969) pointed out that unless parallels between the group and the outside situation can be drawn, then the greater the commitment to the group the more difficult the transfer to outside. The lesson is clear that all groups attempting change in their members should pay a great deal of attention to the application of that change in the everyday world and not generate cohesion by isolating techniques that make transfer difficult. As Miller says, 'to the degree that the means are emphasized the ends may be lost' (1976: 231).

Miller (1976) goes on to argue that in the early stages of a group the members comply with the situation and the group leader (see p. 187 on newcomers) and work to the norms of the group. After a period of time sufficient trust develops between the members of the group, based, so Kelman says, on their identification with the group leader as role model and on an identification with the group that reduces each member's sense of isolation and provides a support system. At this stage, Kelman says, 'the satisfying relationship to the group would become an end in itself rather than a means to further self-examination and insight-producing experiences' (quoted by Miller 1976: 230–31).

But this step is only a stage in the process, the last stage of which is the internalization of new values and behaviours. Once this stage has been reached the new learning becomes the possession of the learner and may be used by him or her as he or she wishes; it is not dependent for its continued existence and utility on the presence of the group, which effected it.

If we examine the evidence from these writers – and there is much more in the same vein – we are compelled to recognize the inherent danger of any isolated, cohesive group becoming an end in its own right for its members rather than means to an end, i.e. effecting internalized change of attitudes or behaviours or both. The concentration by the group on material within the group, the so-called 'here and now' focus, if not balanced by sufficient reference to situations outside the group, particularly in terms of the possible application of what new learning is taking place, may well cause the group to stick at the stage of identification. The consequences are that whatever has been gained in the group can be maintained only within it, and transfer of that learning to other situations will be fraught with difficulty.

It would seem therefore that group-living situations containing some of the following elements would need to plan their application sequence most carefully:

(1) Use of a short-term through-put residential system.
(2) Use of separation and isolation from 'normal' society as an important factor in the design of the system.
(3) Aiming to create cohesive groups within the system as learning or support or insight-creating units.
(4) Development of a set of group norms that are markedly different to those of society at large to promote the aims of the organization.

If the residential system is long-term then the process of re-entry into the normal life of society has a much better chance of becoming part of the process of that system:

'Therefore the most important requirement in obtaining transfer of learning is to generate, along with the knowledge of any specific behavior, the basic skills needed to diagnose new situations effectively and those needed to develop co-operation with others involved to generate the competent behavior appropriate to the situation.'

(Argyris 1967: 220)

Vinter and Galinsky (1974: 290) suggested that three procedures might effectively fulfil Argyris's requirements:

(1) Replication of the external problem.
(2) Group discussion of the external problem.
(3) Initiation and review of external action.

Vinter and Galinsky suggest that, in order to transfer and stabilize changes originating within the group, part of the operation of the group should be to replicate exactly those kinds of problem within the group that members will face when they transfer to the society at large. This will inevitably involve using material that comes up within the group activity and relating it purposefully to problems of re-entry, perhaps using simulation or role-play, bearing in mind that such procedures enhance attachment to the group only if they are seen in a 'game' context.

Group discussion of the re-entry problem is self-evident, and Vinter and Galinsky's third suggestion, that 'group members may be encouraged or required to take action between sessions in order to apply, test or reinforce learning acquired within the group', is equally straightforward.

There is much to recommend that all residents subject to the conditions listed earlier should be given the opportunity to become aware that any changes the residential period has effected will be faced with the problem of re-entry. It should be defined clearly what sources of influence will exist that will tend to run counter to the maintenance of such changes, and the methods of recognition and coping discovered.

Much of what has been discussed here can also be understood in the context of public conformity and private acceptance (see p. 97) in the adoption of safety procedures, i.e. apparent conformity. But what has also been stressed is that the changes that are real are also often fragile, and to expect them to survive in a relatively uncaring or even antagonistic environment is naïve, to say the least. Even if internalization takes place, an extra dimension of how to cope with it in society, in a family or a work group that has a memory and expectations established before the change, is essential.

Golembiewski (1976: 166) suggests that four conditions are more likely to promote transfer and retention of learning from T-group experience; they are:

(1) Learner's status.
(2) Practice for transfer.
(3) The home context.
(4) Degree of involvement in the group.

The common sense of these four conditions is clear. The greater the prestige, status, and power learners have in the situation to which they return from the group, the easier they should find it to implement and sustain their new learning. Learners are in fact more likely to change others because of their confidence and status, than others are to pressurize them to revert. Many residents leaving group-living situations do not have high status, nor do they have power and confidence. One of the main consolidating factors is therefore not available to them.

As noted earlier, part of the preparation for transfer is to practise within the security of the group the situation after transfer as far as it can be known. To rehearse the common problems demonstrably reduces their unfamiliarity and can provide coping techniques that reduce what Golembiewski calls 'the discrepancy between insight and action' (1976: 167).

One of the great problems of transfer is that the new situation 'can encourage the learner to retain his learning, but to partition it off from his behaviour in that context' (1976: 168) – a matter of suppression rather than loss. The new situation has to be one that can encourage the use of the new learning or at least that allows selected parts to be practised. Once more we can see that many leavers in residential situations are not readily going to meet with encouraging 'back-home' situations.

Transfer of learning is greater in those participants who have been well involved in their group, who have received good-quality feedback, and have responded to it in a positive way. Like item (2) this condition is one within the control of the group to some degree, whereas items (1) and (3) are personality and external factors largely outside that control.

Marzillier (1978), reviewing the outcomes of skill training for the mentally ill, covered much the same kinds of idea as we have been noting above. Strictly speaking he was not dealing with learning in a group context but with individual learning, but the problems are markedly similar. In suggesting methods of maintaining new behaviour and generalizing it to real life he quoted Kazdin (1975), who offered seven ways in which this might be achieved:

(1) Rewards used in training should be those that would normally occur in the environment to which transfer is likely, so that the new behaviour will continue to receive the same reinforcing consequences.
(2) Individuals in the transfer situation can be trained to reward the learner in appropriate ways.
(3) When new skills are well established, training and support can be reduced gradually rather than abruptly.
(4) Rewards can be 'thinned' or 'intermittent'.
(5) New behaviour can be developed in a variety of situations and in the presence of several individuals.
(6) New behaviour may be maintained by gradually increasing the gap between its production and reward.
(7) People can be taught to evaluate their own behaviour and to establish criteria for rewarding themselves.

Generalizing learning to situations other than those in which the learning took place is concerned fundamentally with spreading the number of situations and people and in turning the evaluative and rewarding processes from being external to being self-administered.

Not all group-living situations are concerned with a through-put system, and thus the establishment and maintenance of change relate only to the degree of adaptation to the current group-living setting that can be brought into existence. But even group-living systems containing more or less permanent residents are subject to changes in their organization, direction, and management which can pose transfer problems. Indeed the complexity of transfer to a different regime or system without change of location may create problems of confusion, resentment, anger, and withdrawal because much that is known and familiar remains though the individual's existence within it has changed.

The whole process of relocation of new learning has been aptly described as one of 'building bridges', which in other words means linking the two situations. This is done by moving ideas, problems, situations, people, and structures from one end to the other in both directions. Transfer of learning is not so much taking one's baggage from point *A* and setting up at point *B*, which is in different territory, as establishing before moving as many similarities between *A* and *B* as possible.

EVALUATION

There are so many questions to which we have only partial answers, or worse still no answers at all. A basic requirement of being able to ascertain that something works is to be able to measure change, however crudely. This implies setting some base line from which assessments of change can be made. Because this is so difficult, very little research actually measures items of change that are of benefit to the practitioner seeking to know what procedures will produce the outcomes he or she desires; and even smaller quantities of research have been devoted to discovering how well changes stand up after they have occurred, as we have seen.

It has long been a maxim of good groupwork that it is essential to evaluate what occurs because it is only by the slow and painful method of collecting data of what happened over many sessions and many different groups that patterns will emerge showing sequential relationships between the various factors of the group process. Evaluation in these terms is the fundamental part of the consolidation of experience. Granted no two experiences are identical in detail; but they do have similarities, and on a different level of understanding than the immediate they show characteristics that allow them to be categorized and permit general principles to be established.

In considering the transfer of learning I have been discussing mainly the consolidation of learning of those who come into a group-living situation that to some degree exerts pressure for change great or small, over a long or short time, and who are then returned 'back home'. As we have seen, the conditions that predispose to success are difficult to effect. One large sub-group in the residential setting, the staff, does not go through exactly the same process; nevertheless, the ability to consolidate learning and experience is as great a necessity, if not greater, for them as for their residents.

A process that becomes an established practice becomes a tradition that is taught to new entrants and is basically suitable to those situations where it deals with an unchanging intake. But where the intake to the process comprises human beings the fact that they all have in common some major factor – e.g. being old, homeless, or mentally disturbed – can in no way be taken to imply that all the uncommon factors can be ignored. If such differences are denied then the system becomes a processing plant, and the intake is squeezed into the available patterns. In so doing the individual often reaps the benefit of that system, e.g. treatment, at extraordinarily high cost to other areas of his or her existence. Evaluating this situation is merely a matter of establishing how well the processing has gone. Thus those who rebel against the effects the system is having in other parts of their existence are merely recorded as difficult or unsuitable.

A residential system must have prime aims, must have a central function. Given the disparity of entrants to that system and the fact that only some part of their need relates to the system's central aim, then built around the central function should be some capability to be flexible and within limits to design personal programmes. This kind of system requires a much more exacting process of evaluation. It is not enough to record entry and discharge after a relatively calm passage, because the degree of flexibility will demand that a continuing estimate of what is happening should be made. In essence a feedback loop is necessary so that programmes are modified in the light of the effects they produce.

Thus we are looking at two major forms of evaluation: one that on a daily basis allows for monitoring the effect of a programme and for the need to change elements of it in the light of the discovered effects; and one that relates to a much longer time span in which the larger patterns and processes can be seen with the advantage of the perspective of distance.

The immediacy of much work in residential systems, the appalling lack of resources that sometimes exists, and the wide variety of need mitigate against such evaluations taking place and enhance the prospect of the development of routines. Energy is then devoted to maintaining the system. In group-work literature and research it is no accident that the three major areas of behaviour are listed as task-related, mainten-ance-related, and personal security. A group cannot operate to perform any function if it is not maintained not only in being but in effective being. But like all essential behaviours it is possible for maintenance to become the totally absorbing passion of a group to the exclusion of performing the task for which it was formed.

Only evaluation of what is actually happening, taken from as many involved and less involved sources as possible, correlated, and scanned, can produce evidence. Thus an evaluation by the staff of what is happening to the people in their care is a necess-arily biased one and needs to be balanced by an evaluation given by those in receipt of that care and perhaps by others indirectly involved like parents, relatives, and other interested parties. The complex nature of the assessment of effectiveness of a group-living situation can so easily frustrate practitioners into taking short cuts or putting assessment so low on their agenda of priorities that it is seldom given the attention it needs.

Groupwork abounds with stories of workers whose grasp of what was happening in their group was wholly based upon their personal assessment. Change was measured in terms of a 'feeling' that things had changed. No relatively objective criteria of the nature of change are established because there is often no base line against which any form of change could be measured. Thus initial behaviour patterns were not systematically logged, and change was measured against memories of what those initial patterns were like; memory, especially in a busy residential system, is hardly the most reliable of instruments.

The basic fact about evaluation is that it is the sole instrument by which effectiveness in a social system can be measured.

There is no product of a social system that can be measured in terms of quantity or quality as in an industrial process. There is always the possibility that repeated change is due to emotional factors, which may be spurious and mask the fact that feeling and reality have no causal relationship. There is always the possibility also that to measure in some truly objective fashion what change does take place might be so distressing that the system would collapse. Evaluation of group systems does lead nevertheless to a more effective system, however small the movement may be. The prime factor in effective evaluation is recording.

RECORDING

Recording is always a sore point with groupworkers, I suspect because it tends to detract from the enormous pleasure working with a group can give, because it is related to the discipline of making permanent what is in effect ethereal, because it is fundamentally analytical in nature, and because it takes groupwork out of the realms of immediate experience and requires evidence of effectiveness.

There is a strong tendency among people working with groups to be concerned only with the immediate present. They forget or choose to ignore that much of human behaviour is constructed around patterns, habits, routines, and practices, all of which are built up over relatively long periods of time and show subtle gradations of performance when followed in situations perceived as different by the performer. How do psychiatrists, for instance, know that what they are seeing in the clinic is what they would see in their client's home? Their very presence in the patient's perceptual field produces a significantly different performance from what would result from their absence.

Some patterns of behaviour may be so strong that no account is taken by their performer of significant changes in his or her surroundings. But even then this can be truly known only when the pattern has been repeated a sufficient number of times for the probability of its occurrence to become relatively predictable.

Much more subtle changes of behaviour, or those that occur less frequently, are therefore in great danger of being unnoticed or seen as one-off occurrences. Some form of recording is thus essential so that even over fairly long periods of time the large and the small, frequent and infrequent, common and special patterns of behaviour can be seen.

Modern methods of recording group behaviour, e.g. video and audio recordings, while missing nothing in their particular mode or range, are tedious in the extreme to use except in very special circumstances. Each recording has to be scanned, and this can be done only sequentially; i.e. one cannot see a visual recording of a group all at once; much retracking and scrolling is necessary to see patterns of behaviour emerging over the period of the recording. In any case most forms of mechanical or electronic recording are intrusive or hidden and thus pose ethical problems.

There is no genuine substitute for recording made by a recall system operated by the observer trained to relate what he or she sees to a time scale – so that the sequence has a basis of objectivity – and for that recall to be recorded in some permanent form as near as possible to the time of origin. Notes made in this way can be placed side by side and scanned for the emergence of patterns over quite long periods of time. All the individual records are available at the same time and immediately. Good habits can be readily fostered with practice, and I have always discovered what amazing recall groupworkers can achieve in a short time when practice is structured.

Scanning records from several sources relating to the same situation, while more difficult, increases the probability that emerging patterns will bear a more certain resemblance to the occurrence recorded.

Work with groups can be performed at the level of a reasonably pleasant pastime with probable spin-offs in terms of relationships and the generation of good feelings that may be quite gratifying. Or it can be performed as a serious attempt to bring about changes and developments that are not ephemeral. In the former mode, recording is not essential, because the groupworker is 'flying by the seat of his or her pants'; in the latter, it is essential as a method of constantly refining one's understanding of a complex situation and of evolving patterns of behaviour related in terms of effectiveness to a defined aim or aims.

SUMMARY

Learning to work effectively with groups of people either in single small groups or as part of a large organization is a process of constant assessment and experimentation. The basics of human interaction expressed as a series of principles are ubiquitous and form the foundation upon which continuous impositions of analysed and structured experience can be built.

This process of accretion can take place only if there is some more or less permanent record of what happens in group situations. Human memory tends to be short, fallible, and selective. A record is the only way in which long-term developments can be charted, in which consequences that are not an immediate response can be noted and related to the causal situation, and thus patterns of behaviour that would otherwise remain wholly obscure come to be exposed over time.

This is of course an ideal process, largely unattainable in ordinary working situations. However, the benefit of even minimal attempts to consolidate and structure experience are large enough for the effort to be more than worthwhile. But my experience has shown that this benefit has to be demonstrated before people become willing to take on what appears at first sight to be a pedantic task. One thing is certain: without some attempt to consolidate experience in this way the understanding of group behaviour that can be used in a practical situation does not increase, and practice is idiosyncratic and dilettantish. Knowledge that informs practice has to be structured and accessible. It is of little value, however vast its extent, if it is garnered and held in a haphazard fashion. Access to it becomes such a labour that it is often abandoned in favour of habit because the time taken to scan large quantities of unstructured information is not really acceptable.

The simile I have frequently used to demonstrate the point at issue here is the difference between a well-run library and a book stall at a jumble sale. In the former the information about what is available is open and accessible with minimal effort; in the latter, although it may contain some extraordinarily desirable items, no one can know without personally examining every item on offer.

Afterword

Whatever form the training of residential workers takes with respect to the aspects of group living discussed throughout this book, certain intransigent problems need to be recognized. First and most important is the difference between language and the human systems it seeks to describe.

In trying to draw attention to just a small part of any group-living situation, the complexity of interacting systems is not only beyond description but also beyond our ability to grasp. If we take five people talking to one another in a particular room, the conversational group is a focal point at any instant for literally hundreds of influence systems, monitored by the individual's perceptions of the situation. Additionally, the situation itself is feeding new data to each of the five, with the possibility of adding yet more influence systems at different levels of awareness to those already present or at least suggesting probable modification to them.

No wonder therefore that language, however mathematical or complex, cannot hope to do more than describe the more obvious interacting systems, and it can do that for only those systems that are known about or signal their presence.

All through this book I have been trying to illustrate the embedded nature of all systems and the abysmally useless attempts we make to understand social behaviour out of context. Literally nothing has any meaning except as it relates to other things, essentially because it has been brought about by the interaction of many factors, some known and some not. Nothing springs into being whole and complete, owing its existence to nothing; such an entity cannot exist within our ability to understand it. And yet we persist, often for apparently good reasons, in acting as though we could understand such a phenomenon and indeed go so far as to wrench things from their context in order to create a class of isolate phenomena.

Learning about group living most clearly needs — indeed, cannot take place without — some basic understanding of the network of intertwining systems, of events, of memories, of experience, of current perceptions, and so on, underlying even the simplest situation. This is a Herculean task that can never be wholly achieved. But not to try is to consign oneself and one's colleagues and clients to a wholly superficial level of understanding and, if understanding of some kind is the basic requirement of any effective intervention, also to a series of useless or relatively useless attempts to help.

It is essential to get this point understood by anyone who is interested in working with groups; more important than any amount of information about group dynamics or any number of techniques for working with people in groups. Without this basic understanding, the heart and soul will not be in whatever learning takes place. Maier (1967) stressed that successful groupwork practice was more directly the result of what he called 'internal consistency' in the ideas used than of the actual nature of those ideas.

The whole basis of learning about groups is not to discover some quintessential truths but to create a series of constructs about group behaviour that will enable us to make sense, of a kind, out of what occurs in our daily life. If it does nothing else it should serve to make us fully aware of the nature and quality of the information we possess, how it was arrived at, and ultimately the nature and the quality of the decisions that we may make based upon it. One thing the flirtation with computers has made widely understood is that data that is essentially rubbish can produce only decisions based upon it of the same quality.

References

Ainsworth, F. and Fulcher, L. C. (1981) *Group Care for Children: Concept and Issues*. London: Tavistock.

Altman, I. (1970) Territorial Behavior in Humans: An Analysis of the Concept. In L. Pastalan and D. Carson (eds) *Spatial Behavior in Older People*. Ann Arbor, Mich.: University of Michigan – Wayne State.

Amir, Y. (1969) Contact Hypothesis in Ethnic Relations. *Psychological Bulletin* 71: 319–42.

Andrews, E. E. (1972) Therapeutic Interaction in Adult Therapy Groups. In R. C. Diedrich and H. A. Dye (eds) *Group Procedures: Purposes, Processes and Outcomes*. New York: Houghton Mifflin.

Argyle, M. (1969) *Social Interaction*. London: Methuen.

Argyris, C. (1967) On the Future of Laboratory Education. *Journal of Applied Behavioral Science* 4: 147–77.

Aronson, E. (1980) *The Social Animal*. San Francisco: W. H. Freeman.

Ashby, W. R. (1968) Principles of Self-Organising Systems. In W. Buckley (ed.) *Modern Systems Research for the Behavioral Scientist*. Chicago: Aldine.

Bandura, A. (1969) *Principles of Behavior Modification*. New York: Holt, Rinehart, & Winston.

Bateson, G. (1967) Cybernetic Explanation. *The American Behavioural Scientist* 10 (8): 29–32.

Beck, J. C., Buttenwieser, P., and Grunebaum, H. (1968) Learning to Treat the Poor: A Group Experience. *International Journal of Group Psychotherapy* 18 (3): 325–36.

Bednarek, F., Benson, L., and Mustafa, H. (1976) Identifying Peer Leadership in Small Work Groups. *Small Group Behavior* 7 (3): 307–16.

Benne, K. D. and Sheats, P. (1964) The Functional Roles of Group Members. In J. W. Orton (ed.) *Readings in Group Work. Selected Academic Readings*.

Berkowitz, L. and Green, J. A. (1965) The Stimulus Qualities of the Scapegoat. In A. Yates (ed.) *Frustration and Conflict*. New York: Van Nostrand.

Berlin, J. S. and Dies, R. R. (1974) Differential Group Structure: The Effects on Socially Isolated College Students. *Small Group Behavior* 5 (4): 462–71.

Berne, E. (1964) *Games People Play: The Psychology of Human Relations*. New York: Grove Press.

Block, S. (1961) Multi-Leadership as a Teaching and Therapeutic Tool in Group Psychotherapy. *Comprehensive Psychiatry* 2: 211–18.

Blumberg, A. and Golembiewski, R. T. (1976) *Learning and Change in Groups*. Harmondsworth: Penguin.

Bochner, A. P., Di Salvo, V., and Jonas, T. (1975) A Computer-assisted Analysis of Small Group Process: An Investigation of Two Machiavellian Groups. *Small Group Behavior* 6 (2): 187–203.

Bombard, A. (1953) *The Bombard Story*. Trans. Brian Connell. London: Deutsch.

Bonney, W. C. (1974) The Maturation of Groups. *Small Group Behavior* 5 (4): 445–61.

Bowker, D. M. (1984) *The Guardian*. 11 January: 10.

Bradford, L. P., Stock, D., and Horwitz, M. (1961) How to Diagnose Group Problems. In R. T. Golembiewski and A. Blumberg (eds) *Sensitivity Training and the Laboratory Approach*. Itasca, Ill.: Peacock.

Brearley, P., Gutridge, P., Hall, F., Jones, G., and Roberts, G. (1980) *Admission to Residential Care*. London: Tavistock.

Brearley, P., Black, J., Gutridge, P., Roberts, G., and Tarran, E. (1982) *Leaving Residential Care*. London: Tavistock.

Brown, R. (1965) *Social Psychology*. New York: Free Press.

Cartwright, D. (1966) Achieving Change in People: Some Applications of Group Dynamics Theory. *Human Relations* Nov. (4): 381–92.

Cattell, R. B. (1951) New Concepts for Measuring Leadership in Terms of Group Syntality. *Human Relations* 4: 161–82.

Chapple, E. D. and Coon, C. S. (1965) The Equilibrium of Groups. In A. P. Hare, R. F. Bales, and E. F. Borgatta (eds) *Small Groups*. New York: Knopf.

Christie, R. and Geis, F. (1970) *Studies in Machiavellianism*. New York: Academic Press.

Cohen, A. M., Robinson, E. L., and Edwards, J. L. (1969) Experiments in Organisational Embeddedness. *Administrative Science Quarterly* 14 (2).

Collins, B. E. and Guetzkow, H. (1964) *A Social Psychology of Group Processes for Decision Making*. New York: Wiley.

Cowger, C. D. (1979) Conflict and Conflict Management. In *Working with Groups* 2 (4): 309–20..

Crandall, R. (1978) The Assimilation of Newcomers into Groups. *Small Group Behavior* 9 (3): 331–36.

DeLamater, J. (1974) A Definition of Group. *Small Group Behavior* 5 (1): 30–44.

DeLong, A. J. (1973) Territorial Stability and Hierarchical Formation. *Small Group Behavior* 4 (1): 55–63.

Dies, R. R., Mallet, J., and Johnson, F. (1979) Openness in the Co-Leader Relationship: Its Effect on Group Process and Outcome. *Small Group Behavior* 10 (4): 523–46.

Dollard, J., Miller, N. E., Doob, L. W., Mowrer, O. H., and Sears, R. R. (1939) *Frustration and Aggression*. New Haven, Conn.: Yale University Press.

Douglas, T. (1970) *A Decade of Small Group Theory, 1960–1970*. Bristol. Bookstall Publications.

—— (1976) *Groupwork Practice*. London: Tavistock.

—— (1979) *Group Processes in Social Work*. Chichester: Wiley.

—— (1983) *Groups: Understanding People Gathered Together*. London: Tavistock.

Edney, J. J. and Uhlig, S. R. (1977) Individual and Small Group Territories. *Small Group Behavior* 8 (4): 457–68.

Eisenstadt, S. N. (1964) *From Generation to Generation*. New York: Free Press.

Ellis, D. G., Werbel, W. S., and Fisher, B. A. (1978) Toward a Systemic Organisation of Groups. *Small Group Behavior* 9 (4): 451–67.

Eysenck, H. J. and Eysenck, M. (1981) *Mindwatching*. London: Book Club Associates/Michael Joseph.

Feldman, R. (1967) Determinants and Objectives of Social Groupwork Intervention. In J. L. Roney (ed.) *Social Work Practice*. New York: Columbia University Press.

—— (1969) Group Integration: Intense Personal Dislike and Social Groupwork Intervention. *Social Work* 14 (3): 30–9.

—— (1974) An Experimental Study of Conformity Behavior as a Small Group Phenomenon. *Small Group Behavior* 5 (4): 404–26.

Festinger, L. (1950) *Social Responses in Informal Groups*. New York: Harper Bros.

Festinger, L. (1957) *A Theory of Cognitive Dissonance*. Stanford, Calif.: Stanford University Press.

Fisher, A. (1974) *Small Group Decision-Making: Communications and the Group Process*. New York: McGraw-Hill.

Freedman, J. L. (1975) *Crowding and Behavior*. San Francisco: W. H. Freeman.

French, J. R. P. and Raven, B. (1959) The Bases of Social Power. In M. D. Cartwright (ed.) *Studies in Social Power*. Ann Arbor, Mich.: Institute for Social Research, University of Michigan.

Frey, D. E. (1979) Understanding and Managing Conflict. In S. Eisenberg and L. E. Patterson (eds) *Helping Clients with Special Concerns*. Chicago: Rand McNally.

Garland, J. A. and Kolodny, R. L. (1966) Characteristics and Resolution of Scapegoating. In S. Bernstein (ed.) *Explorations in Groupwork*. Boston: National Conference of Social Work.

Garvin, C. D. (1981) *Contemporary Groupwork*. Englewood Cliffs, NJ: Prentice-Hall.

Gauron, E. F. and Rawlings, E. I. (1975) A Procedure for Orienting New Members to Group Psychotherapy. *Small Group Behavior* **6** (3): 293–307.

Gibbard, G. S. and Hartman, J. J. (1973) The Oedipal Paradigm in Group Development. *Small Group Behavior* **4** (3): 305–54.

Gilstein, K. W., Wright, E. W., and Stone, D. R. (1977) The Effects of Leadership Style on Group Interactions in Differing Socio-political Subcultures. *Small Group Behavior* **8** (3): 313–32.

Glasser, P., Sarri, R., and Vinter, R. (1974) *Individual Change through Small Groups*. New York: Free Press.

Glover, J. A. and Chambers, T. (1978) The Creative Production of the Group: Effects of Small Group Structure. *Small Group Behavior* **9** (3): 387–92.

Goffman, E. (1968) *Asylums: Essays on the Social Situation of Mental Patients and Other Inmates*. Harmondsworth: Penguin.

—— (1969a) *Presentation of Self in Everyday Life*. Harmondsworth: Penguin.

—— (1969b) Insanity of Place. *Psychiatry* **32**: 357–88.

Goldbart, S. and Cooper, L. (1976) Safety in Groups: An Existential Analysis. *Small Group Behavior* **7** (2): 237ff.

Golembiewski, R. T. (1962) *The Small Group*. Chicago: University of Chicago Press.

—— (1976) *Learning and Change in Groups*. Harmondsworth: Penguin.

Golembiewski, R. T. and Blumberg, A. (1970) *Sensitivity Training and the Laboratory Approach*. Itasca, Ill.: Peacock.

Gordon, T. (1955) A Description of the Group-Centred Leader. In R. C. Diedrich and H. A. Dye (eds) *Group Procedures: Purposes, Processes and Outcomes*. Boston, Mass.: Houghton Mifflin.

Goroff, N. N. (1971) Social Groupwork – an Intersystemic Frame of Reference. *Journal of Jewish Communal Service* **47** (3): 229–37.

Greening, T. C. (1973) When a Group Rejects its Leader. *Small Group Behavior* **4** (2): 245–48.

Guinan, J. F., Foulds, M. L., and Wright, J. C. (1973) Do the Changes Last? A Six-Month Follow-Up of a Marathon Group. *Small Group Behavior* **3** (2): 177–80.

Hackney, H. (1974) Facial Gestures and Subject Expression of Feelings. *Journal of Counseling Psychology* **21**: 173–78.

Hare, A. P. (1962) *Handbook of Small Group Research*. New York: Free Press.

—— (1973) Theories of Group Development and Categories for Interaction Analysis. *Small Group Behavior* **4** (3): 259–304.

Hartford, M. E. (1971) *Groups in Social Work*. New York: Columbia University Press.

Haythorn, W. H. (1953) The Influence of Individual Members on the Characteristics of Small Groups. *Journal of Abnormal and Social Psychology* **48**: 276–84.

Heap, K. (1977) *Group Theory for Social Workers: An Introduction*. Oxford: Pergamon.

Henriques, J., Holloway, W., Urwin, C., Venn, C., and Walkerdine, V. (1984) *Changing the Subject*. London: Methuen.

Hill, W. F. and Gruner, L. (1973) A Study of Development in Open and Closed Groups. *Small Group Behavior* **4** (3): 355–81.

Hirschman, A. O. and Lindblom, C. E. (1962) Economic Development, Research and Development, Policymaking: Some Converging Views. In F. E. Emery (ed.) *Systems Thinking*. Harmondsworth: Penguin.

Hughes, R. (1980) *The Shock of the New*. London: BBC Publications.

Jacobs, A. and Spradlin, W. W. (1974) *The Group as Agent of Change*. New York: Behavioral Publications.

Janis, I. L. (1972) *Victims of Groupthink: A Psychological Study of Foreign Policy Decisions and Fiascoes*. Boston, Mass.: Houghton Mifflin.

Jones, E. E. and Nisbett, R. E. (1971) *The Actor and the Observer: Divergent Perceptions of the Causes of Behavior*. Morristown, NJ: General Learning Press.

Jurma, W. E. (1978) Leadership Structuring Style, Task Ambiguity, and Member Satisfaction. *Small Group Behavior* **9** (1): 124–34.

Kanter, R. M. (1972) Commitment and Community, Communes and Utopias. In *Sociological Perspective*. Cambridge, Mass.: Harvard University Press.

Katz, D. and Kahn, R. L. (1969) Common Characteristics of Open Systems. In F. E. Emery (ed.) *Systems Thinking*. Harmondsworth: Penguin.

Katz, S. I. and Schwebel, A. I. (1976) The Transfer of Laboratory Training: Some Issues Explored. *Small Group Behavior* **7** (3): 271–86.

Kazdin, A. E. (1975) *Behavior Modification in Applied Settings*. Homewood, Ill.: Dorsey Press.

Kelman, H. C. (1963) The Role of the Group in the Induction of Therapeutic Change. *International Journal of Group Psychotherapy* **13**: 399–432.

Kinze, A. F. (1971) Body Buffer Zones in Violent Prisoners. *New Society*. 28 January: 140–41.

Klein, A. F. (1972) *Effective Groupwork*. New York: Association Press.

Lazarus, A. A. (1974) Understanding, and Modifying Aggression in Behavioral Groups. In A. Jacobs and W. W. Spradlin (eds) *The Group as Agent of Change*. New York: Behavioral Publications.

Lazlo, E. (1972) *Introduction to Systems Philosophy*. New York. Harper & Row.

Levinson, D. A. and Jensen, S. M. (1967) Assertive versus Passive Group Therapist Behavior with Southern White and Negro Schizophrenic Hospital Patients. *International Journal of Group Psychotherapy* 17 (3): 328–35.

Lieberson, S. and O'Connor, J. F. (1972) Leadership and Organisational Performance: A Study of Large Corporations. In A. Etzioni and E. W. Lehman (eds) *A Sociological Reader on Complex Organisations*. New York: Holt, Rinehart, & Winston.

Litvac, E. (1967) Communication Theory and Group Factors. In E. Thomas (ed.) *Behavioral Science for Social Workers*. New York: Free Press.

Lundgren, D. C. (1975) Interpersonal Needs and Member Attitudes towards Trainer and Group. *Small Group Behavior* 6 (4): 371–88.

McArdle, C. G. and Young, N. F. (1970) Classroom Discussion of Racial Identity or How Can We Make it Without 'Acting White'? *American Journal of Orthopsychiatry* 40 (1): 135–41.

McCaughan, N. (1980) The Purposes of Groupwork in Social Work. In P. B. Smith (ed.) *Small Groups and Personal Change*. London: Methuen.

McCullough, M. K. (1963) Groupwork in Probation. *New Society* 21: 9–11.

McGrath, J. I. and Altman, I. (1966) *Small Group Research*. New York: Holt, Rinehart, & Winston.

Maier, H. W. (1961) Group Living: A Unique Feature in Residential Treatment. In *New Perspectives on Services to Groups: Theory, Organisation and Practice*. New York: National Association of Socialworkers.

—— (1967) Application of Psychological and Sociological Theory to Teaching Social Work with the Group. *Journal of Education for Social Work* 3 (1): 29–40.

Mann, R. D. (1967) *Interpersonal Styles and Group Development*. New York: Wiley.

Marzillier, J. (1978) Outcome Studies of Skills Training: A Review. In P. Trower, B. Bryant, and M. Argyle (eds) *Social Skills and Mental Health*. London: Methuen.

Merton, T. (1948) *Introduction to Selected Texts from Mohandas K. Gandhi, 'Non Violence in Peace and War'*. (Publisher unknown.)

Miller, F. D. (1976) The Problem of Transfer of Training in Learning Groups: Group Cohesion as an End in Itself. *Small Group Behavior* 7 (2): 221–36.

Millham, S., Bullock, R., and Hosie, K. (1980) *Learning to Care: the Training of Staff for Residential Social Work with Children*. Farnborough: Gower.

Millham, S., Bullock, R., Hosie, K., and Haak, F. (1981) *Issues of Control in Residential Child Care*. London: HMSO.

Mills, T. M. (1964) Authority and Group Emotion. In W. G. Benne *et al.* (eds) *Interpersonal Dynamics*. Homewood, Ill.: Dorsey Press.

Mitchell, R. R. (1975) Relationships between Personal Characteristics and Change in Sensitivity Training Groups. *Small Group Behavior* **6** (4): 402–14.

Moore, E. E. (1978) The Implication of System Network for Social Work with Groups: Literature and Experience. *Social Work with Groups* **1** (2), Summer. New York: Haworth Press.

Newcomb, T. M. (1957) The Prediction of Interpersonal Attraction. *American Psychologist* **11**: 575–86.

—— (1963) Stabilities and Underlying Changes in Interpersonal Attraction. *Journal of Abnormal and Social Psychology* **66**: 376–86.

—— (1965) Interpersonal Constancies: Psychological and Sociological Approaches. In O. Klineberg and R. Christie (eds) *Perspectives in Social Psychology*. New York: Holt, Rinehart, & Winston.

Northen, H. (1969) *Social Work with Groups*. New York: Columbia University Press.

Norton, R. W. (1979) Identifying Coalitions: Generating Units of Analysis. *Small Group Behavior* **10** (3): 343–54.

Nydegger, R. V. (1975) Leadership in Small Groups: A Rewards–Costs Analysis. *Small Group Behavior* **6** (3): 353ff.

Oshry, B. I. and Harrison, R. (1966) Transfer from Here-and-Now to There-and-Then: Changes in Organisational Problem Diagnosis Stemming from T-Group Training. *Journal of Applied Behavioral Science* **2**: 185–98.

Palomares, U. (1975) *A Curriculum on Conflict Management*. La Mesa, Calif.: Human Development Training Institute.

Paradise, R. (1968) The Factor of Timing in the Addition of New Members to Established Groups. *Child Welfare* **47** (9): 524–29, 553.

Payne, C. (1978) Working with Groups in a Residential Setting. In N. McCaughan (ed.) *Groupwork: Learning and Practice*. National Institute Social Services Library. London: Allen & Unwin.

Pincus, A. and Minahan, A. (1973) *Social Work Practice: Model and Method*. Itasca, Ill.: Peacock.

Raven, B. H. and Rubin, J. Z. (1976) *Social Psychology: People in Groups*. New York: Wiley.

Reddy, W. B. and Lippert, K. M. (1980) Studies of the Processes and Dynamics within Experiential Groups. In P. B. Smith (ed.) *Small Groups and Personal Change*. London: Methuen.

Redl, F. (1942) Types of Group Formation, Group Emotion and Leadership. *Psychiatry* **5** (4): 573–96.

Reisman, D. (1950) *The Lonely Crowd*. New Haven, Conn.: Yale University Press.

Roethlisberger, F. J. and Dickson, W. J. (1939) *Management and the Worker*. Cambridge, Mass.: Harvard University Press.

Rosenbaum, M. (1971) Co-Therapy. In H. I. Kaplan and B. J. Sadock (eds) *Comprehensive Group Psychotherapy*. Baltimore, Md.: Williams & Wilkins.

Rosenthal, R. (1966) *Experimenter Effects in Behavioral Research*. New York: Appleton-Century Crofts.

Rosenthal, R. and Rosnow, R. (1969) *Artifact in Behavioral Research*. New York: Academic Press.

Sabath, G. (1964) The Effect of Disruption and Individual Status on Person Perception and Group Attraction. *Journal of Social Psychology* **64**: 119–30.

Schultz, B. (1978) Predicting Emergent Leaders: An Exploratory Study of the Salience of Communicative Functions. *Small Group Behavior* **9** (1): 109–14.

Schur, E. M. (1979) *Interpreting Deviance: A Sociological Introduction*. New York: Harper & Row.

Schutz, W. C. (1959) *F.I.R.O.* New York: Holt, Rinehart, & Winston.

Scioli, F. P., Dyson, J. W., and Fleitas, D. W. (1974) The Relationship of Personality and Decisional Structure to Leadership. *Small Group Behavior* **5** (1): 1–22.

Shalinsky, W. (1969) Group Composition as an Element of Social Group Work Practice. *Social Service Review* **43** (1): 42–9.

Shapiro, B. Z. (1977) Friends and Helpers: When Ties Dissolve. *Small Group Behavior* **8** (4): 469–78.

Shapiro, R. J. and Klein, R. H. (1975) Perceptions of the Leaders in an Encounter Group. *Small Group Behavior* **6** (2): 238ff.

Shaw, G. B. (1897) *The Devil's Disciple*.

Shaw, M. E. (1971) *Group Dynamics: The Psychology of Small Group Behavior*. New York: McGraw-Hill.

—— (1974) *An Overview of Small Group Behavior*. University Programs Modular Studies. Morristown, NJ: General Learning Press.

Shaw, M. E. and Blum, J. (1966) Effects of Leadership Style upon Group Performance as a Function of Task Structure. *Journal of Personality and Social Psychology* **3**: 238–42.

Sherif, C. W. (1976) *Orientation in Social Psychology*. New York: Harper & Row.

Shostrom, E. L. (1967) *Man, the Manipulator*. Nashville, Tenn.: Abingdon.

Shulman, L. (1967) Scapegoats, Group Workers and Pre-emptive Intervention. *Social Work* **12** (2): 37–43.

Slavson, S. (1953) Sources of Countertransference and Group Induced Anxiety. *International Journal of Group Psychotherapy* **3**: 373–85.

Smith, D. (1978) Dyadic Encounter: The Foundation of Dialogue and the Group Process. *Small Group Behavior* **9** (2): 287–304.

Smith, P. B. (ed.) (1980) *Small Groups and Personal Change*. London: Methuen.

Southwick, P. C. and Thackeray, M. G. (1969) The Concept of Culture in the Neighborhood Center. *Social Casework* 50 (7): 385–88.

Steiner, I. D. (1974) *Task-Performing Groups*. University Programs Modular Studies. Morristown, NJ: General Learning Press.

Sudnow, D. (1967) Dead on Arrival. *Trans-Action* 5: 36–44.

Terhune, K. R. (1970) The Effects of Personality in Co-operation and Conflict. In P. Swingle (ed.) *The Structure of Conflict*. New York: Academic Press.

Thibaut, J. W. and Kelley, H. H. (1954) Experimental Studies of Group Problem-Solving Process. In Gardner Lindzey (ed.) *Handbook of Social Psychology*. Reading: Addison-Wesley.

Thorndyke, E. L. (1931) *Human Learning*. New York: Appleton-Century Crofts.

Tutt, N. (ed.) (1976) *Violence*. London: HMSO.

Vinter, R. D. (1967) *Readings in Group Work Practice*. Ann Arbor, Mich.: Campus Publishers.

—— (1974) The Essential Components of Social Group Work Practice. In P. Glasser, R. Sarri, and R. Vinter (eds) *Individual Change through Small Groups*. New York: Free Press.

Vinter, R. D. and Galinsky, M. J. (1974) Extra Group Relations and Approaches. In D. Glasser, R. Sarri, and R. Vinter (eds) *Individual Change through Small Groups*. New York: Free Press.

Wahrman, R. (1977) Status, Deviance, Sanctions and Group Discussion. *Small Group Behavior* 8 (2): 147–68.

Walker, T. G. (1974) Decision-making Superiority of Groups. *Small Group Behavior* 5 (1): 121ff.

Weinstein, M. S. and Hanson, R. (1975) Leader Experience Level and Patterns of Participation in Sensitivity Training Groups. *Small Group Behavior* 6 (2): 123–40.

Whittaker, J. K. (1974) *Social Treatment: An Approach to Interpersonal Helping*. Chicago: Aldine.

Wiener, N. (1948) *Cybernetics or Control and Communication in the Animal and the Machine*. New York: Wiley.

Wilcox, J. and Mitchell, J. (1977) Effects of Group Acceptance/Rejection on Self-Esteem Levels of Individual Group Members in a Task-Oriented Problem-Solving Group Interaction. *Small Group Behavior* 8 (2): 169–78.

Williams, J. S., Martin, J. D., and Gray, L. N. (1975) Norm Formation or Conditioning? A Study in Divergence. *Small Group Behavior* 6 (2): 141–50.

Williams, R. M. (1947) *The Reduction of Intergroup Tensions*. New York: Social Science Research Council.

Wilmer, H. A. (1966) Free Association of People: Observation on the Changing Constellations in Large Group Meetings. *International Journal of Social Psychiatry* 12 (1): 44–51.

Wilson, G. and Ryland, G. (1948) *Social Group Work Practice*. Boston, Mass.: Houghton Mifflin.

Winter, S. K. (1976) Developmental Stages in the Roles and Concerns of Group Co-Leaders. *Small Group Behavior* 7 (3): 349–62.

Woods, T. L. (1972) Parents Preparation Group. *Comparative Group Studies* 3 (3): 201–11.

Wright, F. (1976) The Effects of Style and Sex of Consultants and Sex of Members in Self-Study Groups. *Small Group Behavior* 7 (4): 433–56.

Wright-Mills, C. (1959) *The Sociological Imagination*. New York: Oxford University Press.

Yalom, I. D. (1970) *The Theory and Practice of Group Psychotherapy*. New York: Basic Books.

Zaleznik, A. and Moment, D. (1964) *The Dynamics of Interpersonal Behavior*. New York: Wiley.

Zinberg, N. E. and Glotfelty, J. A. (1968) The Power of the Peer Group. *International Journal of Group Psychotherapy* 18 (2): 155–64.

Name Index

Subject Index